HAUNTED INDIANA

Mark Marimen

Thunder Bay Press

Published by Thunder Bay Press
Designed and typeset by Maureen MacLaughlin-Morris
Publisher: Sam Speigel
Cover design by Lynda A. Bass
Cover layout by Adventures with Nature, East Lansing, MI
Printed by Baker Johnson, Dexter, MI

ISBN: 1-882376-38-2

Printed in the United States of America

04   4 5 6 7 8 9

Other titles in the *Thunder Bay Tales of the Supernatural* series:

Chicagoland Ghosts
Haunted Indiana II
Haunted Indiana III
Haunts of the Upper Great Lakes
Michigan Haunts and Hauntings

TABLE OF CONTENTS

Dedication

Dedicating one's first book is a daunting task. This book is dedicated first of all to my wife and daughter who unselfishly supported me in its writing. I love you. This book is also dedicated to my parents who filled my life with silent applause and who never let on that it was odd to have a son who was hooked on ghost stories. You are the best and I owe you more than I could ever tell..

Finally, this book is for Jay, who inadvertently started off this whole business.

Note

In the writing of this book, careful attention has been given to collecting legends that have, in many instances, been told for generations. In some cases, scenes have been recreated in the telling of these old legends which may not reflect historical events. The author makes no claim as to the exact historical authenticity of any of the legends represented in this book. Additionally, some of those who have chosen to tell their stories in this book have requested that their names be changed to protect their privacy. In these cases an asterisk (*) has been added to their name the first time it is mentioned.

FOREWORD

It never ceases to amaze me how coincidental life can be. At odd moments you find yourself in a place you never thought you would be, perhaps doing things you might never have thought that you would do, and you ask yourself, "How did this happen?" Then you start to reflect back on the series of events that brought you to that point in your life. Eventually, you trace it back to a small, seemingly insignificant event that led to a slight change in your life, then another and another, until a part of your life has shifted direction.

Tonight I sit in my living room, on a cold, windswept October night (the perfect kind of night for ghost stories), preparing to send off the first draft of a book on Indiana ghost stories. I look back at all that has gone into this project and all that remains to be done. I look back at a lifetime fascination with ghost lore, and I wonder, "How in the world did all this start?"

As I trace it back, I guess I am here because of two seemingly unrelated and insignificant facts from my past. The first is that I was born in the first week of September, 1960. The second is that my brother, Jacob, like many older brothers, was born a sadist. Those two facts for me explain why I am writing this book.

The date of my birth figures into my history because of the fact that as I was growing up in Merrillville, Indiana, the youngest of three children, early September was also the first week of school. Since this invariably was a very hectic time at my house, this meant that there was neither time nor energy for me to have a birthday party with my friends during my young years. In truth, this absence never bothered me, since my parents more than made up for it with the largess of our family get-togethers. I never thought about the fact that I had never had a traditional birthday party with my friends until the age of eleven, when I finally decided that there was profit to be made in utilizing this fact.

I then started on a conniving and whining campaign with my parents, until at long last, they relented and announced that I could have a few friends over the last week of August for a pool party and sleep out in the back yard, all as a substitute for a birthday party.

And so it was, that from the age of eleven to about fifteen, every year, during that last golden, precious week of summer, my friends and I would gather in my back yard to howl and laugh and celebrate the sweetness of summer, made especially sweet because it was dying before our very eyes. Afterward we would sit around a campfire, built in what had formerly been my sandbox, and roast hotdogs and watch the night draw closer, and laugh at adolescent dirty jokes that none of us fully understood. But that did not matter because we were young, the fire was bright, and the summer was sweet.

It was into this setting that my brother Jacob came one night. It was late in the evening and we sat hunched around our fire watching the stars slowly fade into existence above us. My brother suddenly appeared out of the deepening twilight, and sat among us. He did not come because he craved our company. He did not come out of a gesture of good will. No, my brother came to scare us to death, and this he nearly did.

Jacob told us stories. Ghost stories. Not the classical stories that came out of thick books at the library, but REAL stories. TRUE stories. He knew them to be true because they had all happened quite near to us—some even to 'friends of his friends.' He told us some of the stories that appear in this book—and I believed them every one.

I should note that ordinarily I would not have believed my brother had he told me that Tuesday follows Monday. But there was something about sitting around a fire, in that last bittersweet week of August, that wove a spell around me. Perhaps it was innocence, or gullibility, or just something in the air of that night. Perhaps it was the magic of that last sweet week of summer—only the twelfth summer I had known.

But whatever the cause, I believed my brother as he told us stories of things that go bump (not to mention moan and screech) in the night. When he was finished, sleep did not come easily that night, and when the morning came the sun shone down on a different world for me. A world more mysterious, and somehow more romantic. A world dappled by sunlight and warmth, but with deep shadows, where ghosts lurked and spirits whispered among the leaves. I woke to an exciting and wonderful world, all because of some perfectly "true" things that happened right near here.

Of course, time has passed. The years have worn away the veneer of my innocence and naiveté. I am a professional now, as well as a husband and father. Day in and day out I deal with the realities of life. Yet somehow, at odd moments, I find myself longing to be twelve years old again, sitting around a campfire, listening to my brother tell tales. I long to return to a world where ghosts lurk and spirits whisper among the leaves.

Perhaps that is why I have collected these stories. Please understand that they are neither fact nor fiction. Most are neither total fabrication nor academic histories of events. Some are classic Indiana legends handed down for generations, and some are new stories to be considered 'legends in the making.' Neither quite actuality nor utter fabrication, they belong to the nether world of literature called 'folklore,' and as such are simply intended to amuse, and entertain.

Well—perhaps they are meant to do one thing more.

It is my hope that they will transport you back to a time in your life when you were twelve years old, sitting around a campfire, listening to stories. To rediscover, for just a moment, the sweetness of the innocence and wonder that come from the hearing of them.

Be warned! If it is great fiction or parapsychological truth that you seek, you might well look elsewhere. But, if you simply want to spend some time around this campfire, then pull up a chair and settle back, and let me tell you of some strange stories of our Hoosier state—all 'perfectly true' and as it just so happens—they happened right near here . . .

PART I
CLASSIC GHOSTS

Diana of the Dunes

The Legend of Stiffy Green

A 1957 Chevy. The movie *Casablanca*. The beauty of Marilyn Monroe. Some things are just classics. Even in the realm of ghost lore, some stories are simply classic. Old stories of unsettled spirits and specters destined to walk the earth for all eternity. Remnants of the past who reach out from history to grip our lives in some way. In Indiana, there are some stories that simply will not be forgotten. Shades of our shared past not content to lie quiet. Here are some classical ghost stories from the domain of Indiana ghost lore.

DIANA
OF THE DUNES

It was a fisherman who first saw her as he cast his line into the surf. She emerged from the waves just as the first rays of dawn began to break through the early morning mist on Lake Michigan. Though the spring morning was a chilly one, she wore no covering except the long damp hair that streamed down her back. She was a small slender woman with dark hair and skin that was tanned brown from the sun. As the stunned fisherman watched, she ran from the water, turned for a moment to look back at the lake from which she had emerged, and then she was gone, leaving behind her only a set of footprints in the sand, and one fisherman, barely able to believe what he had seen.

The year was 1915, and the place was just north of Chesterton, Indiana, in an area now occupied by the Dunes State Park. In those days, long before the commercial value of the lake front had been realized, much of the area between Gary and Michigan City was uninhabited wilderness. While the lake front was frequented by fishermen and swimmers escaping the summer heat, few ever ventured into the dense forest that hugged the lake front for miles. It was, in fact, the perfect place for someone seeking to escape the confines of human society. Perhaps that is what drew this enigmatic young woman to the area in the first place.

The name of the first fisherman to see her is now lost in the dust of time. One thing that is known is that he did not keep silent about what he had seen. By the summer of 1915 the story began to spread throughout the surrounding communities concerning the beautiful 'hermit of the dunes.' Soon a number of fishermen and swimmers began to report seeing her. She was shy and elusive, avoiding contact with the outside world. Those who were able to get close enough to speak to her found her timid and skittish, evading questions and offering little information about herself. All she wanted, she said, was to be left alone.

Despite Diana's wish for anonymity, her fame in the surrounding communities began to spread. The mystery surrounding her identity and origin only seemed to stimulate the local thirst for knowledge about her. Stories concerning her were told and retold, until folk tale became legend, and legend took on the guise of fact. Soon her legendary persona was larger than life.

In the tales told around the kitchen tables and across the clothes lines of northwest Indiana, she became a stunningly beautiful creature, roaming the hills and woods of her domain always totally nude. In the collective imagination of the area she became more than real—she became a goddess. Further, since her real name was unknown, she was given the name of a goddess—Diana.

With tales such as these filtering through the community, it is only understandable that Diana of the Dunes soon began to attract visitors. Within a year of taking up residence in her new home, the privacy and quiet of the dunes area began to be disturbed by an onslaught of curious sightseers, seeking to catch a glimpse of the bronzed goddess that they had heard so much about. Though elusive as ever, Diana was eventually tracked down to an abandoned fisherman's shack where she slept and kept her meager belongings. Most intruders were warned off by a stern voice and the wild dog that she had adopted. A few, however, were more persistent, and managed to even speak to the "Goddess." Among these was a reporter dispatched from one of Chicago's leading newspapers. Diana's fame it seemed had escaped even the bounds of the Hoosier State.

Why she granted the interview with a reporter remains a mystery. Perhaps she just wanted to lay to rest the rumors told about her. Perhaps she was hoping that by telling her story she might satisfy the curiosity of those who wished to disturb her solitude. Whatever the reason for her candor with the reporter, the newspaper story only served to increase her popularity with the local populace. It did however, clear up much of the mystery concerning the origin of this enigmatic figure.

Her name, she said, was Alice Mable Grey. She had been born into a prominent family in nearby Chicago. Far from being the unlearned hermit of local folklore, Diana, or Alice as she now may more properly be called, was a cultured, genteel

Indiana Dunes
Photograph by Kris Harrison

woman. She had traveled extensively, was well-educated, and had graduated with honors from the University of Chicago. After graduation she had taken a position as an editorial secretary at a nationally-known astronomy magazine.

What had driven her from the comforts of society and into the solitude of the lake shore wilderness has never been precisely known. At the time, it was said that a broken love affair had caused her to leave her life behind. More recent research has suggested that failing eyesight had made it impossible for her to continue in her exacting line of work. Whatever her reasons, in 1915 she packed a few of her belongings and leaving family and friends behind her, made her way to the Indiana dunes. She picked this area apparently because she had occasionally visited the lake shore with her family as a child and was fond of its rugged beauty.

After sleeping for several nights on the beach, she discovered a fisherman's cottage, long abandoned and neglected. Here she made her home, moving in the few books and writing utensils that she had brought with her. Her days were spent bathing in the often chilly waters, hiking in the woods, and reading. She was inventive and resourceful, living off the land around her. What needs the land could not fulfill were met by her occasional hikes to Miller, Indiana, where she would buy provisions and borrow library books. She was said to have kept extensive journals of her time in the dunes, warding off the loneliness of her life by communing with the nature around her.

In 1920, this loneliness was broken in a very different way. A man joined her in her rugged life. His name was Paul Wilson, an unemployed boat builder from Laporte with a checkered past. Though rumored to be an 'unsavory character,' Wilson did much to improve the condition of Alice's ramshackle cottage. Tall and strong, Wilson was a commanding presence. He helped Alice make ends meet by doing occasional odd jobs for local residents and selling the fish that he caught. Perhaps more importantly, his presence helped discourage the curious from disturbing the peace of Alice's life. For a short period of time their life was a tranquil, apparently happy one, despite the occasional sightseer.

However, by the early 1920s, civilization was moving closer and closer to their once-secluded home. Eventually, Alice and her companion moved several miles to the east, hoping to avoid the onrush of society. Even here, however, Paul and Alice would find no peace. In 1922, tragedy struck. Hikers found the partially burned body of a man on the beach. An autopsy revealed that he had been strangled by someone with great strength. Though the body was too badly burned to allow an identification, let alone provide any evidence as to the man's killer, local residents were quick to point an accusing finger at a likely suspect—Paul Wilson.

Wilson was held by local police for questioning, despite his loud protests of innocence. In fact, Wilson inadvertently served to deepen the mystery by blaming a 'gun toting hermit' who had been frequenting the area recently. No such hermit was ever discovered and not enough evidence was found to charge Wilson with the crime.

Wilson was eventually released to return to Alice, but the incident marked the end of an era for the pair. Soon thereafter, Alice and Paul Wilson moved to nearby Michigan City, Indiana, where they eked out a living by selling handmade furniture and taking in sewing. It was during their stay in Michigan City that Mrs. Wilson, as she now called herself, bore her 'husband' two daughters. While their life was less rugged in their new home, it was not a happy one. Recent research into the life of Alice Grey has suggests that not only did Alice and her family live in abject poverty, but Alice was also subject to frequent beatings at the hands of Paul Wilson. Time was running out for the woman who had once been called 'Diana of the Dunes.'

On February 11, 1925, shortly after the birth of her second daughter, Alice Grey died in her home. The official cause of death was listed as uremic poisoning, a common complication of pregnancy in those days. The diagnosis seemed logical at the time, but we now know that in addition to uremic poisoning, Alice's condition was complicated by repeated blows to the abdomen and back. She was buried at Grace Park Cemetery in Gary.

However, in a final twist of irony, it was later revealed that instead of the grave plot that her family had purchased for her, Alice was buried illegally in a mass grave by an unscrupulous cemetery employee. As one researcher has noted: "In death, this sensitive and gentle woman found, at last, the privacy she sought so desperately in life."

Thus ends the story of Alice Gray. Or does it?

Some might say no. It is said that in death Alice still returns to the dunes she loved so well in life. Over the years more than one person has reported seeing a ghostly figure of a woman running along the sand by the light of the full moon, or emerging nude from the surf, only to vanish in the air before their eyes.

In 1972, a park ranger patrolling the dunes one evening is said to have reported seeing a dark figure of a woman emerge from the surf. The ranger approached the woman to tell her that there was no swimming allowed after dark, but as he drew within ten feet of her she turned, glanced at him for a moment, and then vanished. Occasional hikers in the woods behind the dunes area have told stories of glimpsing a strange-looking woman traipsing across the hills, only to disappear leaving no trace of her passage.

If, indeed, the ghost of Alice Grey continues to roam the lake front, one might only wonder what she thinks of the changes that the years have brought to the area. Of course, there are those who scoff at such stories, but still, around the kitchen tables and clothes lines of northwest Indiana, it is said that Diana of the Dunes still roams the land she loved so well.

It was a fisherman who first saw her, as he cast his line into the surf just before dawn. She emerged from the waves just as the last light of the full moon disappeared behind the mist rising off the lake. Though the early spring morning was a chilly one, she wore no covering except for the long damp hair that streamed down her back. As the stunned fisherman watched, she ran from the water, turned for a moment to look back at the lake from which she had emerged, and then she was gone, seeming to evaporate into the mist. This time, she left no footprints behind her.[1]

THE LEGEND
OF STIFFY GREEN

Dogs, so the old proverb says, are man's best friend. While some might take issue with such conventional wisdom, for many other people, dogs sometimes become more than mere pets — they become intimate friends and lifelong companions. And, if the tales told in the vicinity of Highland Lawn Cemetery in Terre Haute are to be believed, at least one man has taken his relationship with his dog beyond life, and into the realm of Indiana ghost lore.

John Heinl was a well-known and beloved figure around Terre Haute in the early years of this century. An elderly gentleman without immediate family, Heinl spent much of his time taking long strolls through the town, his favorite pipe in hand, greeting and visiting his many friends throughout the growing area. Everyone, it seems, knew John Heinl, and the little dog that was the constant companion on his wanderings. Indeed, it was rare that the elderly gentleman was seen in public without the company of his bulldog, Stiffy Green, walking protectively by his side.

According to the legend of Stiffy Green, the dog's unusual name came from the awkward gait of the animal, coupled with the fact that unlike most members of his breed, Stiffy was possessed of piercing green eyes. Indeed, new members of the community were sometimes startled when, stopping to speak to the affable Mr. Heinl, they found themselves under the close scrutiny of his small companion with the arresting green eyes. Stiffy Green was known to be fiercely protective of his master, never allowing strangers too close to him. It was even said that as John Heinl slept, Stiffy Green slept at the foot of his bed, guarding him in his sleep just as he did during the daylight hours.

In any case, the pair seemed inseparable, one never out of sight of the other. John lavished love and affection on his little dog, and Stiffy returned his affection by providing his master with company, comfort, and the companionship needed to ease the loneliness of his elderly years.

It was death that eventually parted the two boon companions. In 1920, the aged Mr. Heinl died in his sleep. While his passing caused much sadness among his many friends in the community, it was his dog Stiffy that was his chief mourner. The dog was inconsolable, refusing to leave his master's side even during his funeral and entombment in the family crypt at Highland Lawn Cemetery.

After the funeral service ended, several of Heinl's friends and distant relatives tried to leash the dog in order to lead it away. At first, the dog kept his would-be rescuers away by snarling and showing his teeth. Even in death, Stiffy refused to abandon his beloved master. Eventually, the dog was captured and taken to the home of one of John Heinl's distant relatives in Terre Haute. However, even in his new home Stiffy refused to be consoled.

Within a week the dog was reported missing. He was found shortly thereafter sitting mournfully by the door to the Heinl family mausoleum, patiently guarding the eternal sleep of his master. Again the dog was captured and returned to his new home, only to disappear once again. Over the next several months, this became routine. No matter how securely Stiffy Green was guarded or chained, eventually the little dog would escape the confines of his new home, only to be found several miles away, at the door to the Heinl family crypt.

In time, Stiffy Green's new masters gave up trying to keep the dog at home and allowed him to take up residence in the cemetery grounds. At first, workers there tried to bring food and water to the solemn little animal, but these were refused with a snarl and a grimace from those flashing green eyes. For weeks, Stiffy Green sat nearly motionless at the entrance of the Heinl tomb, seeming to challenge anyone from entering. Through rain and cold and darkness, Stiffy Green stood resolutely at his post outside the tomb, as loyal as ever to his master within.

And it was here that his body was eventually found. Time, weather, and lack of nutrition had eventually taken their toll. As word of the dog's death spread, a number of John Heinl's old friends gathered to discuss what should be done with the animal's body. While some recommended that it should simply be discarded, others suggested that it would only be appropriate to allow the animal to be entombed next to his master and friend.

A fund was established and the body of the dog was transported to a local taxidermist who stuffed the remains and transformed his dead body into the unnerving semblance of life. The dog was placed in the sitting position he had maintained for months outside the Heinl tomb. The eyes were left open, with brilliant green glass eyes put in place of the real ones. When the grisly job was completed, the body of Stiffy Green was placed inside the Heinl tomb, next to the crypt of the master he had served so long and so well. It seemed that his service to John Heinl was at last completed.

But perhaps not quite completed. Several months after Stiffy Green took his place in the Heinl family mausoleum, a maintenance worker was leaving the cemetery grounds early one warm fall evening. Just as he was packing his car for the ride home, he heard the excited bark of a small dog coming from the direction of the Heinl family crypt. Since the presence of wild dogs was, of course, discouraged by the cemetery work force, he quickly decided to investigate.

As he neared the precincts of the Heinl mausoleum, suddenly the sound became clearer, and the frightened workman stopped in his tracks. Much to his horror he realized that the sound he was hearing was a familiar one. He had heard it frequently, months before, in this very spot. It was the barking of Stiffy Green.

Then, as suddenly as it had begun, the barking stopped. Summoning all of his courage, the workman crept closer to the grave site and stared at the mausoleum through the line of trees that surrounded it. He heaved a sigh of relief. There was nothing unusual around the crypt. Deciding that this had been nothing more than the barking of a stray dog, or perhaps the product of his imagination, the workman turned and began to walk back toward his car.

Then something else attracted his attention. Out of the corner of his eye he caught the movement of a figure, or a pair of figures, in the distance. He turned once again and stared with horrified fascination at the sight before him. Through the twilight of early evening, he saw, walking quietly along the fence that separated Highland Lawn from the surrounding community, the figure of an elderly man smoking a pipe. By his side, there padded silently the figure of a small dog. All of this, of course, was enough to unnerve the unfortunate workman. But there was one further aspect to the scene that caused his blood to chill: even from a distance, he could clearly see that the dog's eyes sparkled bright green.

Since that fateful day in October 1921, legend has it that many people in the vicinity of Highland Lawn Cemetery have reported hearing the barking of a dog coming from within the confines of the cemetery grounds at odd hours of the day and night. A few have even reported seeing the figure of an elderly man, walking on cool autumn evenings, strolling amidst the windswept leaves. While their descriptions of the figure do vary slightly, they all agree on one point: walking serenely by his side is the figure of a small bulldog with green eyes — eyes now peaceful and content, since dog and master have been reunited beyond death itself.

> Dogs, so the old proverb says, are man's best friend. For many other people, dogs sometimes become more than mere pets — they become intimate friends and lifelong companions. And, if the tale of John Heinl and Stiffy Green is to believed, at least one man has taken his relationship with his dog beyond life, and into the realm of Indiana ghost lore.[2]

PART II
THE OLD SCHOOL
SPIRIT

The Return of the Gipper

The Faceless Nun of Foley Hall

Higher education has long been a point of pride for Indiana. The Hoosier state can lay claim to any number of colleges and universities. Large and small, each of these institutions of higher learning has its own unique history and tradition.

Part of that tradition, in many cases, is the campus ghost story. From one end of the state to the other, it seems that nearly every college has, buried deep within its heritage, a story of a campus ghost or spirit. Many tales have been told in dimly-lit dorm rooms of dark deeds and inexplicable events.

Contained within the next few pages are but a few of the many stories told of Indiana's colleges. Stories new and old that give new and eerie meaning to the term 'the old school spirit' . . .

THE RETURN
OF THE GIPPER

If one were to assemble a list of Indiana colleges and universities (a prestigious list to be sure), a place of honor would have to be afforded the University of Notre Dame. Founded in 1830, Notre Dame has risen to be one of the premier universities in the United States. For over 150 years, the name of Notre Dame has been synonymous with excellent academics, an outstanding student body, and most particularly, collegiate football – and George Gipp – the 'Gipper.' It can be said without fear of contradiction that the spirit of George Gipp has woven itself into the tapestry of American sports. However, if the stories handed down for generations on the Notre Dame campus are to believed, perhaps Gipp might have left more of himself to Notre Dame than his name and legend. Perhaps it is his unsettled spirit that walks the corridors at Washington Hall.

If, as some have suggested, college football is a "second religion" in America, then Notre Dame would have to be its Mecca. Though many colleges throughout the United States can claim strong gridiron credentials, no school in the nation can boast of a longer or more vaunted football history than Notre Dame. Names such as the "Four Horsemen," Hunk Anderson, and Joe Montana have made their way from the pages of Notre Dame history and into the annals of American football legend.

No name, however, has become more legendary than the name of the great George Gipp. Known nationally as the "Gipper," Gipp's story was already well known when it was forever branded into American tradition by Ronald Reagan, who played Gipp in the 1940 movie *Knute Rockne, All American*.

Like many sports legends before him, George Gipp's beginnings were inauspicious. He was born on February 18,

1895 in Laurium on the Keweenaw Peninsula of northern Michigan. The seventh of eight children, Gipp's early life hardly marked him for greatness. As a child, Gipp excelled neither on the sports field nor in the classroom. In school, he was known as a lackluster student noted more for his frequent absences than for his academic achievement.

Though tall for his age, Gipp eschewed organized sports as a child. However, this aspect of his life began to change in 1910 when Gipp entered Calumet High School. In his first fall semester at Calumet, Gipp tried out for the school basketball team and was given the starting position as point guard. Here for the first time his athletic prowess began to shine. Though raw and undisciplined, Gipp showed great speed and agility and an uncanny, almost ruthless, competitive spirit.

However, Gipp's academics were still a sore point. Though naturally bright, Gipp's study skills and commitment to academics seemed nonexistent. Instead, during his final years of high school, Gipp was noted primarily as a disciplinary problem and an avid prankster. His high school principal later recalled that during Gipp's senior year, his chief duties, aside from school administration, were the "once a month routine expulsion of George Gipp."

Though later biographies would suggest otherwise, there is no clear record that George Gipp ever actually graduated high school. Instead, Gipp spent much of his last year of high school at local pool halls and betting parlors, as well as at the local YMCA where he would occasionally become involved in informal baseball games. Though never participating in organized baseball, Gipp had played since the age of eleven in sandlot games and was known for his fire and ability. Ironically, it was to be baseball that finally started Gipp on his road to greatness.

On a hot afternoon in the summer of 1916, Gipp encountered an old acquaintance, Wilber Gray, on a street corner in Laurium. Gray was a graduate of Notre Dame who was playing semiprofessional baseball in Elkhart, Indiana. Having seen

The "Gipper"
Courtesy of University of Notre Dame Archives

Gipp's baseball prowess, Gray mentioned to Gipp that he should consider trying to get a baseball scholarship at Notre Dame. Reportedly, Gipp replied "No, I'm too old to try school again—besides, I don't have any money."

Gray, however, was not so easily discouraged. Several days later, having contacted his alma mater and borrowed the money for the train fare to South Bend, he accompanied Gipp to the station and saw him off. Though no one involved had any idea at the time, an American football legend was in the making.

In early September, Gipp was accepted as an incoming freshman at the University of Notre Dame. His first few weeks on campus were uncomfortable ones for Gipp. He was older than most of the other freshman and he was utterly destitute of funds. While he maintained passing grades in his classes, he seemed aloof and disinterested to professors and fellow classmates alike. Indeed, Gipp seemed ready to leave Notre Dame several times before fate took a hand in the autumn of 1916.

One sunny fall afternoon, Gipp accompanied another freshman to the football practice field to while away some free time. As they leisurely kicked the ball back and forth, they did not realize that they were being watched intently from the sidelines by a stocky middle-aged man smoking a cigar. The man was Knute Rockne, fabled football coach for the 'Fighting Irish.' As the boys tired of their game and began to walk toward their dormitory, Rockne approached Gipp. Years later, Rockne would recall their first meeting.

"What's your name?" I asked. Indifferently, the boy replied "Gipp, George Gipp. I come from Laurium, Michigan."

"Played high school football?" I asked.

"No," he said, "don't particularly care for football. Baseball's my game."

"Put on a football suit tomorrow," I invited, "and come out with the football scrubs. I think you'll make a football player."

From such humble meetings history is made. Gipp appeared the next day on the practice field and soon became a starter for the Notre Dame football team. From the beginning, he was recognized as a football phenomenon. Indeed, in his four years at Notre Dame, Gipp went on to redefine what a football player could be and vaulted college football squarely into the national spotlight.

During his tenure on the Notre Dame gridiron, Gipp helped lead his team to twenty consecutive football victories and two Western Championships. Playing both offense and defense, Gipp excelled at every aspect of the game. In his career he ran the ball for 2,341 yards and passed for 1,769 yards. He ran for twenty-one touchdowns and threw another seven touchdown passes.

However the end was not far away. It has been observed that sometimes the star that shines the brightest often fades the most quickly. The end for George Gipp came in November 1920. After a game against Indiana University, Gipp began to show signs of a slight cold. Confined to bed for most of the next week, Gipp rose the next Friday to lead his team in a winning effort against Northwestern University. Though his performance in the game was, as usual, exemplary, it was clear to one and all the Gipp was not well. On Tuesday morning, November 23, Gipp was admitted to St. Joseph's Hospital suffering from pneumonia.

For the next several days, as Gipp's condition worsened, Notre Dame, and indeed, the entire nation held its breath. Daily reports on his condition were printed in newspapers from Los Angeles to New York. A bevy of newspaper and radio reporters camped in the lobby of the St. Joseph's Hospital waiting for word on the ailing star.

Despite consultation with leading specialists and the best ministrations of the hospital doctors, Gipp's condition continued to deteriorate. On Sunday, December 12, doctors summoned Gipp's family and Coach Rockne to his bedside. Pale and weak, Gipp motioned Rockne to him and spoke the words that would forever seal his fate as an American legend.

"I've got to go Rock. It's all right. I'm not afraid. Some time, Rock, when the teams up against it, when things are wrong and the breaks are beating the boys — tell them to go in there with all they've got and win one for the Gipper. I don't know where I'll be then, Rock, but I'll know about it and I'll be happy."

It was tender moment, later immortalized by Ronald Reagan on film. On Tuesday morning Gipp went into a coma and early on the morning of December 15, 1920, the "immortal" George Gipp slipped into death.

On December 17, the entire student body of Notre Dame and most of the residents of South Bend turned out to see the casket of Gipp being loaded onto a train that would ultimately take the football legend to his final resting place in Calumet, Michigan.

Commenting on the students' final farewell, one reporter wrote, "As though by unspoken command a hat came off here and there, and in a flash the crowd was bareheaded. Silently, with almost defiant faces, the students gazed at the departing form of their idol. Thus ends the career of George Gipp at Notre Dame."

Owing to the gravity of the situation, the reporter's comments were understandable. Subsequent events, however, might well cast a shadow of doubt on his conclusion. In fact, if one were to listen to the tales whispered throughout the years in the vicinity of Washington Hall on the Notre Dame campus, one might begin to question if something of Gipp was left behind at his beloved Notre Dame.

Washington Hall sits squarely in the center of the Notre Dame campus. It is a small, dark, neo-Gothic building that has served for many years as the performing arts center for the college. It has, in turn, been home to the university band, orchestra center, and for the last several decades, the university theater. The high pointed roof without and dark staircases within lend the hall an ambiance conducive to things dramatic, theatrical, and even mysterious.

In the early years of this century, however, Washington Hall was the home to several student apartments as well. Indeed, after fire destroyed much of the campus in the late 1800s, the decision was made to place student rooms in all of the major campus buildings to help relieve the overcrowding of the dormitories. It was decided that because fire and security

Exterior of Washington Hall, University of Notre Dame, circa 1920. Courtesy of University of Notre Dame Archives.

alarms were not in use at the time, the students in each hall would serve as human alarms in case of fire or break-in. Students were housed in several small apartments on the upper level of the building and were supervised by a 'proper,' or dormitory supervisor who lived on the first floor. It was up to this individual, usually a brother from the Order of the Holy Cross, to watch over the building and to impose university discipline upon those living within its walls.

In its time, Washington Hall has been home to a great many students including a future Dean of the Notre Dame Law School and several leaders of business. While university housing records from the time are unclear, legend has it that Washington Hall was also the home to George Gipp during his last semester at Notre Dame.

Further, the tale holds it was Washington Hall that contributed to Gipp's untimely demise. According to the story, Gipp, who was notorious for flaunting university rules, had been caught coming in past student curfew several times that semester. The proper, a stern monk named Brother Maurilius, had repeatedly warned Gipp and finally threatened that the next time he came in late he would face disciplinary proceedings that would eliminate him from the sports program. For once, Gipp seemed to take the threat seriously.

For a short period he was careful to make his appearance before the 11:00 p.m. curfew. However, in mid-November Gipp again found himself ambling back to campus from a night in town after the official curfew time. As he walked towards Washington Hall, the clock on campus struck the midnight hour and Gipp remembered the venerable brother's threat. Rather than risking the ire of Brother Maurilius, Gipp rashly decided to sleep on the steps of Washington Hall instead. Though mild for November, the night was still chilly and damp, and according to legend, when Gipp awoke the next morning, he felt the first chills and sore throat that would later grow into pneumonia and ultimately, take his life.

The story of Gipp sleeping on the steps of Washington Hall is, of course, the stuff of legend. Little can be learned about the veracity of such a tale. However, what is more clear is the mysterious events that began in Washington Hall immediately after the death of Gipp. Events that were linked, in the minds of all those involved, with the death of the fated star.

The events in question started just after the students returned from Christmas break in the first days of 1921. The first to notice something strange going on in the place was band student Jim Clancy, who was alone in the band room on the first floor practicing a difficult trumpet piece for an upcoming concert. As he later related the experience, he was taking a break from his practicing when he heard a strange sound coming from the other end of the room. Investigating, Clancy quickly discovered that the sound, which he described as a kind of "low moan," was in fact emanating from a tuba stacked along the far wall. Then, as suddenly as it began, the sound abruptly ended. Thinking it odd, Clancy quickly picked up his music and turned to leave, only to have the sound come once again from the instrument. As he later declared, "That horn was playing itself!"

Fearing the ridicule of other band students if he told his strange story, Clancy decide to keep it to himself. Within a few days, however, others began to hear the sound too. Joe Shanahan was the first resident to hear the sound several nights later as he was attempting to sneak back into the dormitory after hours. As he passed the band room on his way up the stairs, a low moan came out of the dark air and seemed to fill the building. Later, Shanahan would recount that as he turned and started toward the direction of the sound, he saw a saw a sort of "gossamer haze" floating in the band room. Wasting no time in making his escape, Shanahan bolted upstairs to his room, only to find the other residents of the hall asleep, oblivious to the sound that had seemed to fill the night.

If, on that occasion the residents of Washington Hall were unaware of the phenomena occurring around them, they would soon no longer have that luxury.

Several nights later, Harry Stevenson, a student who lived in Cadillac Hall, was visiting friends in Washington Hall. As the dreaded 11:00 p.m. curfew drew nearer, Stevenson bade farewell to his friends and began to descend the steps down toward the main entrance of the hall. As he came abreast of the first floor landing, he heard the sound of a musical instrument, this time a bugle, float through the darkened hall. Suddenly the music ceased, to be replaced by what he later described as a "weird howling moan." So startling were the sounds that Stevensen collapsed in hysterics on the steps, to be found several minutes later by his friends who had heard the sound and his cries. Immediately, the lamps were lit and the band room searched, only to find no one, or nothing, there.

The interior of Washington Hall, University of Notre Dame, circa 1920. Courtesy of University of Notre Dame Archives.

Strange as these occurrences were, they were just the beginning. Soon the eerie sounds in the dead of night became a regular occurrence at Washington Hall. Moreover, they were now accompanied by the sound of footsteps. One resident at the time described hearing the sound of an instrument at midnight, followed by running steps coming directly up the staircase toward the student living quarters. Immediately he and several other students ran to the landing and though they heard the footsteps approaching they saw nothing on the stairs.

Now the phenomena began to widen in scope. Doors began to slam when there was no one in the vicinity. One student, leaving his living quarters, felt a hand push him while walking down the steps past the band room. Residents began to have objects disappear from their rooms, only to have them turn up again in odd places.

Needless to say, these strange phenomena soon began to attract the attention of the entire student body. Soon it seemed everyone on campus was claiming an encounter with the famed ghost of Washington Hall. One student even claimed that as he was passing Washington Hall one night, he saw a ghostly figure on horseback ride through campus and up the steps to Washington Hall, only to disappear on the doorstep. The figure on the horse, he claimed, was none other than George Gipp! This is how the ghost became known as the spirit of Gipp.

Soon the faculty became aware of the stories. A group of students, led by "Doc" Conell, decided to stay overnight in the band room to disprove the stories. By their own accounts, they were rewarded by hearing the customary unearthly sounds in the room as well as by seeing a filmy substance appear in one corner of the room. One student reportedly was pushed from his cot by unseen hands.

A carnival atmosphere soon began to pervade Washington Hall as more and more curious students tried their hand at 'laying' the ghost. In the midst of this, however, only one person remained unaffected and apparently unconvinced. The staid Brother Maurilius remained unabashedly skeptical about the entire event. He claimed to have never heard or seen anything out of the ordinary and seemed willing to write the entire event off as student pranks and mass hysteria.

Such was the case until one night when he was awakened from his sleep by a sound he later described as "a cross between a crash and an explosion" coming from the stairway. Thinking something heavy had dropped or fallen, he ran to the stairway only to see nothing there. Then, suddenly, he too heard the mournful note, floating out from the band room.

Convinced that he was the victim of a hoax, Brother Maurilius ran to the band room and searched it, but found it empty. He next went to the rooms of the student residents, only to find them asleep. Rudely awakening his young charges, Brother Maurilius demanded an explanation, but none was afforded. "Brother," said one student, "now you get what we have been living with for these past weeks. Are you convinced yet?"

He was definitely convinced. The next morning Brother Maurilius appeared in the office of Father Charles O'Donnell, provincial head of the Order of the Holy Cross, and demanded something be done. Later that day, Brother Maurilius was seen leading O'Donnell on a tour of the building, and though he seemed skeptical, he promised a full investigation.

What was done, if anything, at the good brother's behest is unknown. The stories of the ghost of Washington Hall seemed to quiet some in succeeding years, only to be revived again in 1945 when residents reported hearing footsteps on the roof of the building in the dead of night and having lights mysteriously turn themselves off and on.

The years have brought changes to Washington Hall. The band room has since been converted into classrooms and an experimental theater. Since the 1950s, Washington Hall has ceased to house students on a regular basis, yet unsettling phenomena have continued to be experienced there. One student, working late one evening setting lights for an upcoming production, was startled to see a light bulb he had just screwed in unscrew itself before his eyes and crash to the floor beneath his ladder. Another student, who served as caretaker of Washington Hall one summer reported hearing doors slam and seeing lights turn themselves off and on for no apparent reason.

In the mid seventies, several students decided to investigate the curious phenomena of Washington Hall for themselves. They broke into the building late one night, carrying with them an array of photographic and recording equipment. Setting the equipment on the stage, one student went to the light switch next to the stage to turn on some lights. However, the light switch refused to stay in the "on" position. "I would turn it on, and in a second it would flip itself back over to off, leaving us in darkness," he later noted.

Just then, another student noticed that the flash on his new camera began firing on its own accord. As though to complete the moment, the student said that an unearthly groan that seemed to come from everywhere at once filled the auditorium. Completely shaken, the students fled, never to bother Washington Hall and whatever resides there again.

Not all brushes with the Washington Hall spirit have been so intimidating however. For some students the ghost has been benign and even helpful. In the late 1970s, Lori Pratt Wright was in a play produced at Washington Hall. One night she and several cast members decided to stay late and contact the apparition. After play practice was over, one student hid in the catwalks while the director secured the building for the night. Then, when the building was dark, the cast member climbed down and made his way to a side entrance of the theater where Lori and several other cast members waited in the shadows. Once inside the students climbed onto the stage and lit candles. One student produced a Ouija board and three of the participants placed their fingers on the planchette.

"We asked it if there was anyone in the hall that wanted to speak to us," Lori now recalls, "and the planchette immediately slid to the letters 'S' and 'G' and then slid over to the part of the board that reads 'Goodbye.'" Wondering what such a missive might mean, the students re-asked the question, only to receive the message "S G— Goodbye" again. Now suddenly unsure of themselves, the students decided to abort their seance, packed up their belongings and silently exited by the side entrance.

"As soon as we were out," Lori says, "we looked back and saw a weird light shining through the theater's window. Then it was gone, but in a second it appeared again in the stairwell, coming toward the door we had just left. We all dove into the bushes just as the door opened – and a Notre Dame security guard stepped out. 'S-G.' Security Guard. I think whatever was there was trying to keep us from getting in trouble."

Today, Washington Hall sits quietly amid the splendor of the Notre Dame campus. The current director of Washington Hall says that while he occasionally hears odd noises, he believes them to be just the customary sounds of an old building. "If there is a ghost at Washington Hall, I have yet to meet him – George Gipp or no!" he says.

Yet the stories continue. Throughout the years, other possible explanations for the haunting have been put forward. Some have suggested the ghost is that of a steeplejack killed in the construction of the building. Others tell of a student killed while working on a play. However, sooner or later most of these stories come back to George Gipp, the legendary 'Gipper.'

Few would contest that George Gipp left his mark on American sports, and on Notre Dame itself. Some, however, wonder if he perhaps has left something more – a mischievous spirit that will forever make life interesting at Washington Hall.

> *For over 150 years, the name of Notre Dame has been synonymous with excellent academics, an outstanding student body, and most particularly, collegiate football – and George Gipp – the 'Gipper.' The spirit and legend of George Gipp has woven itself into the tapestry of American sports. However, if the stories handed down for generations on the Notre Dame campus are to be believed, perhaps Gipp might have left more of himself to Notre Dame than just his name and legend.[3]*

THE FACELESS NUN OF
FOLEY HALL

Should old acquaintance be forgot,
Or pass beyond recall?
Our hearts say no, so kudos go,
to dear old Foley Hall.

I lived in Foley in my youth
(the dates I can't recall)
And I for one
knew growth and fun
in stately Foley Hall.

And every person at these woods,
From greatest to the small
Has tales to tell
that weave the spell
of famous Foley Hall

The faceless nun,
the attic dark
The spiral staircase tall
The chapel, classrooms
courtyard too
All Part of Foley Hall"[4]

For some reason, colleges and universities have long been recognized as repositories of ghost lore and legends. Tales are handed down from class to class, generation to generation, until these stories become woven into the tapestry of academic tradition. Indeed, for many institutions of higher education, the "campus ghost" has become as much a part of college life as the smell of musty library books and ivy clinging to granite walls.

Such is the case with St. Mary of the Woods College, a Roman Catholic women's college near Terre Haute. The history of St. Mary of the Woods is a rich one. Indeed, the roots of this academic institution can be traced back to the year 1840, when Mother Theodore Guerin, S.P. (Sisters of Providence) and five other nuns left their motherhouse in Ruille-sur-Loire, France, to venture across the Atlantic. Eventually, their journey ended in the wilderness of what is now central Indiana, near a small settlement on the banks of the Wabash known as Thrall's Station. Through cold midwestern winters and hot summers, these dauntless women worked to overcome countless hardships in order to bring culture and religion to the wilderness.

Eventually, a Catholic mission was founded in a wooded glen not far from town. Shortly thereafter a religious community began to take shape and in 1846 the first Catholic women's college in the United States was founded. Despite the rural surroundings, the concept of higher education for women quickly caught on. By 1860, the college had grown to the point that a more permanent structure was needed to house the school and its inhabitants.

It was in that year that the foundation was laid for what would ultimately become a massive structure, first called "St. Mary's Academic Institute." Later, as the college grew, so did its central edifice, renamed "Foley Hall" after one of the superior generals of the Sisters of Providence.

The next 130 years would see amazing changes at "The Woods," as it has affectionately become known. From its rustic beginnings, St. Mary of the Woods would evolve into a graceful campus of tree-lined streets, wooded vistas, and numerous buildings, most reminiscent of European architectural styles. But it was always Foley Hall that seemed to dominate the campus community. Surrounded on all sides by buildings of lesser stature and history, Foley Hall became the grandam of the college. It became, it seemed, an institution unto itself. In its time, this gothic structure would serve her college as dormitory, classroom facility, chapel, infirmary, cafeteria, and interestingly, an art studio. With its austere sense of quiet grace and elegance, Foley came to serve as the centerpiece of the college and surrounding community. Generations of women came to her doors for learning and growth, and each in turn left her, promising never to forget the time spent there.

The exterior of Foley Hall.
Courtesy of St. Mary of the Woods College Public Relations Department.

The original cornerstone of Foley Hall, laid in 1860, bore the inscription "Wisdom hath built herself a house." Judging from the ranks of women who passed through her halls, it seems fair to say that wisdom did indeed reside within her stone walls. However, if the legends surrounding this beloved structure are to be believed, so did something else. Something darker and more mysterious. Something at once pitiful, yet also sinister — anonymous, nameless, and, quite literally, faceless.

In truth, no one knows the real origin of the legends surrounding the faceless nun, as she came to known. However, most indications point back to the early part of this century when Foley Hall was being used primarily as a classroom facility, with a substantial part of the second floor being used as an art studio. Today, the tale is whispered that a young novitiate nun came to work there as an art instructor. Being quite an accomplished artist herself, this young woman whiled away her free time by doing portraits of her fellow sisters. So renowned were her artistic endeavors that it was eventually suggested that she attempt an artist's greatest challenge: a self portrait.

Soon the work was begun. As many artists do, she began her work by painting what she could readily see — the blue drape that would form the backdrop of the painting, then slowly her clothes and shape took form. Since the face was the most critical and most difficult aspect of the work, it was reserved for last.

So great was the challenge of this endeavor that soon the artist become consumed with her work. Late into the night she would paint by gaslight and shadow. Often the morning would find her slumped in a chair in the second floor studio, sound asleep, her paintbrush still in hand. As days grew into weeks the painting continued to take shape, but still the face remained untouched, waiting it seemed, until the last moment.

Then suddenly tragedy intervened. Before the first feature of the face had been put to canvas, the young nun was struck down with a debilitating illness. Perhaps it was one of the many contagions that swept through the countryside in the early 1900s. Perhaps it was simply the strain of long days and nights in the art studio finally taking their toll. Whatever the cause, the young woman was found one morning collapsed before her faceless work.

She was carried downstairs to the infirmary, but despite the best ministrations of her fellow sisters, she died a few days later. Death had intervened before she had been able to complete her greatest work with the addition of her face. Her body was quietly interred the next day in the private burial ground on campus. The unfinished painting was moved to a storeroom adjacent to the second-story art loft, leaving only paint spatters and dust behind . . . and perhaps, if the legends told are true, an unquiet spirit with unfinished business at Foley Hall.

Through the years any number of people have claimed encounters with the faceless nun, though the best documented experiences came from Sister Esther Newport, who taught in the art department from 1931 to 1964. Although Sister Esther has been deceased for a number of years, she did relate some of her encounters with the faceless nun to Dawn Tomaszewski, a student reporter for *The Woods*, the campus newspaper.

In the resulting article, Sister Esther related a number of experiences she had over many years. The first hint of 'trouble' at Foley, she recalled, came late one cold night, when Sister Esther was working in a small room on the second floor of the building. Sister Esther knew that she was not alone in the building that night, for working in the art studio to the rear of the second floor was a girl named Isabel who was finishing an art project. As the hour grew late, Sister Esther decided to check on Isabel's progress. Quietly she made her way down the long hall that led to the art studio, only to be shocked to find Isabel standing outside the doorway of the art studio. Sensing that something was wrong, Sister Esther asked the girl what was the matter.

"I'm sick and tired of that nun coming around," replied Isabel, visibly agitated. Thinking it strange that another sister could be in the building without her knowledge, Sister Esther asked Isabel to describe the nun in question.

"I don't know," Isabel replied. "She always stands between me and the light—not only that, but she leaves when I try to speak to her and I can never see her face." Curious as her experience was, this was not be the last time that Isabel would encounter the enigmatic figure.

Several weeks later, Sister Esther entered the art studio to find Isabel working on a watercolor project. "Did you find the nun that was looking for you?" Isabel inquired. "She was here just a minute ago."

Puzzled, Sister Esther replied that she had seen none of her fellow sisters in the building. "What did she look like?" asked Sister Esther. Somewhat abashed, the girl replied, "I really do not know — she always stands between me and the light so that I can't see her face."

Thus was born the legend of the faceless nun. While the student Isabel was the first person to encounter the phantom of Foley Hall, she was by no means the last. Soon other students began to report strange confrontations with the mysterious presence. One morning Sister Esther met two more female students in the second floor art gallery who reported glimpsing the silent figure of a nun gliding through the room. Apparently assuming that the sister must be looking for Sister Esther, the two sought her out and reported "a strange nun is looking for you." Again perplexed as to whom the anonymous sister might be, Sister Esther asked about her appearance.

At first the girls seemed reluctant to describe her, haltingly commenting that the sister had pleats down the front of her dress in the manner of nuns from a number of years before. When pressed about her appearance further, the girls grew more reticent, until one of the girls, Catherine, blurted out, "You are going to think that I am crazy sister, but she didn't have any face."

After the first two incidents with Isabel, Sister Esther had been inclined to write the entire problem off as one student with an over active imagination. Now, however, she began to suspect the something more inexplicable might be occurring. This feeling was reinforced several weeks later during a figure drawing class that Sister Esther was teaching in the studio. As Sister Esther sat in one corner of the room silently observing her students working on their sketches, she was startled to see a girl on the far side of the room looking toward the windows and apparently talking to thin air. Not knowing quite what to think, Sister Esther approached her from behind and asked her if there was a problem. At the sound of Sister Esther's voice, the student, a girl named Celine, jumped visibly and said: "But sister, what are you doing there? You were right next to me a moment ago!"

The next incident occurred about a week later, during the very same class period. In the midst of a lecture, Sister Esther found her words interrupted by a loud "swishing" sound coming from the floor. So loud was this sound that it became impossible to continue her lecture. As one of the girls in the class would tell her granddaughter years afterward, "We all thought it sounded different—but for me, it sounded exactly like someone was sweeping the floor with one of those big straw brooms we used to use at home." After much speculation, the class decided that the noise must be originating from some plaster repairs being done on the ceiling of the classroom below. Later investigation, however, revealed that no such repairs were underway in the building.

Such experiences were far too interesting to be kept secret for long on a college campus. Soon the stories of the faceless nun were sweeping through the campus and surrounding community. Much to Sister Esther's surprise, other members of the college began to report previous ghostly encounters in Foley Hall. One sister whom Sister Esther described as a "stolid German nun from Jasper" reported being disturbed by phantom footsteps approaching her from behind several times while she was working in the studio. Finally, the imperturbable sister rather testily told the spirit, "Go away and don't bother me—I'm busy." Perhaps something in her authoritative demeanor might have intimidated even a spirit, for the footsteps disturbed her work no more that night.

An even stranger occurrence happened one night when Sister Esther and a friend were alone in the lofty old studio. Sister Esther, it seems, had been engaged for some time doing the illustrations for a childrens' bible. Her friend, who worked for a publishing firm in Chicago, had come to review the illustrations. As they looked at the canvases that were finished, Sister Esther walked behind a large painting in order to turn it so that her friend could see the work. As she looked up, she saw that her friend had turned her back to her and was talking to someone — or something — that Esther could not see. Sister Esther, by now aware of what might be happening, spoke gently to the woman who immediately jumped and turned full circle to face her. "Are you all over this place? You were just in the corner!"

Sister Esther tried to comfort the visibly shaken woman and the two sat down to discuss what had happened. Clearly, the question of shadows were dismissed since a 1,000 watt fixture flooded the room with harsh light. As the two sat and spoke about the strange vision, suddenly the woman gasped and pointed in the direction of the painting Sister Esther had just turned around. "Why there she is again," said the woman. "There is the sister I saw before." Perplexed, Sister Esther watched the woman's finger as it followed an unseen presence from the center of the room into a supply closet where, the woman said, the figure simply "melted into the doorway."

Strange as the incident seems, it looms even more remarkable in light of further discoveries at Foley Hall. Years later, the walls of the art room supply closet were ripped down, and the remains of a stairway were found that once had linked that part of the building with the lower section, where the nuns had once been housed.

By now the rumors sweeping the campus had turned ominous, and students began to avoid classes held in the building, let alone coming to the facility at night. Sister Esther, sensing that something should be done, arranged to have a mass said in the chapel "for special intentions," which were, in truth, to quiet the unruly specter that had taken up residence in Foley Hall. After the mass was said, the spirit seemed to quiet somewhat, but throughout the succeeding years, girls venturing into the building would report catching fleeting glimpses of a strange sister in the garb of long ago.

In 1987, Foley Hall was leveled in order to make room for a more modern classroom facility. With her went 147 years of history, tradition and pride.

But who knows that there might also have gone the unquiet spirit of a young nun, who had lost her identity nearly a century before at stately Foley Hall.

The original cornerstone of Foley Hall bore the inscription "Wisdom Hath Built Herself a House." Judging from the ranks of women who passed through her halls, it seems fair to say that wisdom did indeed reside within her stone walls. However, if the legends surrounding this beloved structure are to be believed, so did something else. Something at once pitiful, yet also sinister— anonymous, nameless—and quite literally—faceless.[5]

PART III
GHOSTS AROUND THE HOUSE

The Ghostly Colonel of Shadowwood

The Spirits of Forest Hill

Things That Go Bump in the Night

The tradition of the haunted house is the bread and butter of ghostlore. But the popular image of the classically haunted house as an old mansion with creaky doors and dark corridors does not always apply. Nestled unobtrusively within the state of Indiana are many homes that can boast their own private haunts. New and old, large and small, each story is as unique as the home it surrounds.

Here are three stories from Indiana's legion of haunted houses. Two are in classic old homes and one in a modern suburban dwelling. These are but a sampling of the many homes in our state that are said to be inhabited, not simply by the living residents of the Hoosier state, but by spirits from another day and time. Spirits that walk the halls at night, making their presence known in some subtle, and not-so-subtle ways.

They are meant to be enjoyed. Surely they have no connection to your life and experience. But on the next windy night, as the rain pelts against the windows and your home echoes with what you hope is just the settling of the foundation, you might well begin to ask . . . could it be?

THE GHOSTLY COLONEL
OF SHADOWWOOD

Ghostly legends are not always attached to the kind of places that one might think of as especially "spooky." Indiana can boast such unlikely haunted spots as a modern airplane hanger and a new hospital facility. Clearly, many of the spots that legend would connect to ghost lore do not fit into the stereotypical picture of a brooding old mansion surrounded by dark woods. One haunted locale in the Hoosier state, however, not only meets this definition of a haunted house, but far exceeds it – Shadowwood.

If ever there was a mansion that looks haunted it is "Shadowwood," located amidst the rolling, wooded countryside just south of Vincennes, Indiana. Even its name conjures up images of mystery and the supernatural, and the home and estate itself do nothing to alter this impression. Indeed, Shadowwood can well brag of one of the most persistent and well-documented ghosts in the annals of Indiana ghost lore.

As one travels south and west from Vincennes, gradually the Indiana landscape begins to transform itself. The unbroken scenery of flat midwestern plains and farm fields give way to gently rolling hills and shaded valleys, spotted in places with deep woods and glens. Just outside the quaint town of Frichten, the estate of Shadowwood sits atop one of these wooded vistas overlooking the surrounding countryside. The entire estate lies shrouded in an atmosphere of intrigue and the uncanny. Indeed, venturing up the twisting drive that leads to the estate, with the huge oak trees hugging the road on either side, it is easy to feel that one is being transported into another place and time. Then, at the final curve in the road, one catches the first glimpse of the mansion itself.

The singular old house sits on the summit of the knoll, overlooking most of the thirteen-acre estate and the 250-acre forest that surrounds it. The mansion fairly speaks of gentility and old world charm. Inside, its eighteen rooms are richly appointed with a stunning sweeping staircase, high vaulted ceilings and hardwood floors and trim. Complete with its tall stone pillars and large front and back porches, this stunning relic of a more genteel time looks strangely out of place in central Indiana. Indeed, the architecture seems to have been borrowed from the antebellum south, although, as will be noted, its history has a distinctly "Yankee" flavor.

It is both interesting and ironic that this southern revival mansion today sits on the land occupied by Shadowwood estate. This is because the land itself first became noted as an area that was embroiled in tensions generated between the North and South. During the period leading up to the outbreak of the civil war, the area surrounding what is now Shadowwood was a hotbed of sentiment and fervor on both sides of the issue.

During these turbulent days passions ran high on both sides of the slavery issue in Indiana. Among the most vocal were the abolitionists who were staunch supporters of freedom for all slaves and of northern sovereignty. Rose Hill, a lovely farm which was once a part of the Shadowwood estate, was a meeting place for the abolitionists. Legend says that the farmhouse even served as a way station for the underground railroad. It is said that the house contains hidden rooms that were used to hide runaway slaves on their way northward to Canada and freedom.

Perhaps more surprisingly there was also considerable support for the southern cause among the inhabitants of the area. Although a bit more covert, these southern sympathizers had equal passion for their cause. Ironically, the spot that these partisans chose for their secret meetings was a wooded glen directly opposite the Rose Hill farm, on the very hill on which the Shadowwood estate now sits. It was here that they would hold their clandestine meetings and bonfires. As word of their gatherings began to leak out, the hill became known as "Rebel Hill."

After the war between the states had run its terrible course, both Rose Hill and Rebel Hill grew quiet and serene once again. Years later, it was the very peacefulness of the place that drew Colonel Eugene C. Wharf to the area to build his home. Wharf, a decorated hero of the Spanish American War, sought to build a showplace for the community, where he could quietly live out his retirement years.

He chose "Rebel Hill" because of its secluded location and the breathtaking view it afforded of the countryside that surrounded it. No expense was spared in the construction of the mansion. Skilled craftsmen were brought in from all over Indiana to work on the expansive home. Well aware of the

Exterior of Shadowwood Estate
Photograph courtesy of Sigma Pi Fraternity International

history of the hill, Colonel Wharf placed a flag pole directly outside the front door of the home, and every morning he personally would raise the stars and stripes to proclaim his allegiance.

Wharf's dream of building a showplace for the community was certainly realized. Within a few short years, grand receptions were held in the home, hosting some of the most powerful and influential people in the state, and even the nation. According to local legend, the guest lists to these exclusive affairs included members of the Vandenberg and Carnegie families, as well as various governors, legislators, and statesmen of the day.

With the death of Colonel Wharf, the estate of Shadowwood passed into the hands of Vincennes University. In 1963, the estate was given over to the Sigma Pi Fraternity, who have since used the property as their national headquarters. While much time has passed since Colonel Wharf owned Shadowwood, the mansion today remains much the same as it did at the time of its construction. Perhaps that is why, as some believe, the long-dead Colonel still walks the halls of this splendid residence.

An amazing number of people who have lived and worked at Shadowwood claim to have had encounters with its resident ghost. However the Colonel's ghost, as it has come to be known, seems to have taken a particular liking to Mrs. Becky Shermacher, who worked there from 1979 through 1987.

While Becky admits to having heard of the strange tales associated with Shadowwood shortly after beginning to work there, she did not think much about ghosts at first. Then, in late 1987, Becky found herself in the small basement of Shadowwood late one evening copying material for a large mailing the next day.

Having copied the necessary material, she turned off the copy machine and walked across the basement to begin the task of collating the copies. As she began to organize the material, she suddenly heard the familiar click of the copy machine being turned back on, followed by the whir of a copy being run through the machine.

Startled, Becky spun around in the direction of the noise, just in time to see a single copy fall into the return tray. Then the machine fell silent once more. Stranger still was the fact that even though there was nothing in the machine to be copied, the paper that came out was black, as though an intense light had been shining down into the machine. Reflecting back on the incident, Becky now recalls that "it was exactly at that moment that I knew it was time to get the heck out of that basement. I grabbed those papers and ran out of the house as fast as I could."

While this was Becky's first encounter with the 'Colonel,' it was not to be her last. Indeed, it seems that the ghost of Shadowwood began to evidence some fondness towards Becky. Soon Becky began to encounter evidence of the ghost's presence with regularity, especially when she happened to work late at night in the office portion of the house. "It happened pretty regularly," she now recalls almost nostalgi-cally. "You would turn on a light at night and go into the next room only to have the light turn itself off. This happened when I knew very well I was alone in the house. Once, when I was alone in the house, I even heard someone call my name. I heard it quite clearly. I thought it was someone playing a joke until I called over to the house where the men were staying and accused them of playing a joke on me. They seemed to be genuinely puzzled by the whole thing."

In time, Becky came to feel secure working around the presence that she felt around her at Shadowwood. "It was like having someone there watching over you," she remarks. The Colonel did indeed seem to be watching over Becky, as evidenced by an incident that occurred late one night when she arrived to work in the office. As she got out of her car, she noted that the lights were out, since the last co-worker had long since gone home. It was only as she neared the door that she realized that it would be difficult to unlock the front door because her arms were full of papers.

As it turned out, she did not have to. As Becky stood on the front porch fumbling for the key in her pocket, the handle moved and the front door swung open before her. Shocked, she carefully peered inside, but there was only darkness and silence within. Thinking once again that she was the victim of a practical joke, she turned on all the lights in the house and searched closely for the perpetrators, but to no avail. She was alone.

As fantastic as Becky's story may sound, she is by no means the only person to encounter whatever it is that seems to inhabit Shadowwood. Larry Rivera remembers many such brushes with the 'Colonel.' Larry worked as a field representative for the fraternity at about the same time as Becky. While his job required extensive time on the road, when not visiting college campuses, Larry and several other men lived in a small house adjacent to the mansion at Shadowwood. It was from this perspective that Larry was able to observe some of the strange goings-on at Shadowwood when no one was in the building.

Frequently, lights would suddenly come on in different parts of the building late at night. Many times, these lights would appear in a section of the house that had once been used by Colonel Wharf as his private study. At least once, Larry and several others were shocked to see every light in the house suddenly turn on at the same moment. Bravely, they ran toward the house to investigate, but before they could open the front door, the lights simultaneously shut off. Subsequent investigation revealed all doors to the house locked and no one within.

While watching the ghostly antics at Shadowwood from a distance was no doubt unnerving enough for Larry, he also had many firsthand experiences with the ghost. The most frequent of these experiences involved papers that were being worked on suddenly disappearing from plain view, only to reappear later in some unlikely spot. "Invariably," Larry says, "this was accompanied by coffee cups in the vicinity suddenly turning ice cold."

While Larry and his friends tried to rationalize these events as absentmindedness and cold drafts in the old house, other events were not so simple to ignore. The most dramatic of these were the sound of ghostly footsteps that were occasionally heard proceeding up the sweeping central staircase of the home. According to Larry these footsteps sounded at all hours of the day and night, sometimes occurring when the office was filled with workers. Even more disconcerting was the reaction of Blackie, the cat, who had become the office mascot. Whenever the phantom footsteps were heard, the animal would race to the stairs, hair standing straight up on its back, and then stop short. Its eyes seemed to follow something up the stairs that no one else could see.

While some of these incidents occurred to only one or two people in the dark of night, others happened in broad daylight in the presence of many reliable witnesses. Despite the comparatively spectacular nature of some of these manifestations, they were just the tip of the iceberg. The Colonel's ghost made his presence known to a number of people who worked in and around the Shadowwood estate. In the early part of this decade, Mrs. Jeanne Leppert, an editorial secretary for the Sigma Pi newsletter, arrived at Shadowwood one weekend afternoon with some visiting friends. It was her intention simply to show off her unusual workplace since her friends had never seen the estate. As it turned out, they may have found out more about Shadowwood than Jeanne intended.

As they toured the home, Jeanne and her friends plainly heard the sound of water running from the sink in an upstairs bathroom. "It was plain as day," she said. "I could hear the water turn on, run for a moment, and then turn off. Then, in a minute, the whole thing would repeat itself. It was especially weird because I knew for fact that there was no one in the building—or even the whole estate for that matter."

Summoning all of her courage, Jeanne climbed the long staircase to the upper floor and went into the bathroom, only to find the water off. Upon closer examination, however, she could see the sink was wet. "It was a small thing," she said, "but it got to me. We knew that we were in the house alone. There was absolutely no way anyone could have been in the building without my knowing it. We even searched the place afterward, but there was no one there, and there was no way anyone could have gotten in or out without our seeing them. It was just strange. I really do not like to work here alone anymore."

Other ghostly sounds have been heard resounding through the old house. One Sigma Pi field representative who worked there in the late seventies reported coming into the house early one hot summer evening to hear the sound of a party going on in the main ballroom upstairs, where Wharf had once entertained his guests. "It was incredible," he remembers. "I could hear music and voices and the sound of glasses clinking. I tore up the stairs just as fast as I could. I stood outside the doors to the room, which were closed, listened for second and then threw them open. As soon as I opened those doors, the sound was gone, and the room, of course, was empty. Then I tore down the stairs as quick as I had come up them, and left the house. I even forgot what I had come for. It didn't matter to me at that moment. I ran back to the house where the field reps stayed and yelled to one of the guys, 'You won't believe this — the Colonel is back, and he's brought friends.'"

Though any number of people claim to have experienced the presence of the ghost they call the 'Colonel,' only one may have caught a glimpse of him. One morning in 1980, a young field representative came to the building early to work on a project before leaving for a week-long trip. As he approached the main entrance, his mind very much on getting his task accomplished before leaving on his trip, a movement in an upper floor window caught his attention. "I looked up at the window that was in the main room upstairs," he said, "and I could clearly make out the face of an old man staring out. He was not looking at me. I think he was just looking out at the entire estate. I cannot say for sure, but in my mind I think it was the Colonel, just coming back to Shadowwood to check up on us. If it was him, I hope he liked what he found."

Perhaps, indeed he did, because while the manifestations still continue at Shadowwood, they have slowed down somewhat in recent years. Still however, workers will report the occasional sound of footsteps or the odd light that turns itself off for no apparent reason.

> Clearly, whatever or whoever it is that walks the domain of Shadowwood, heard but unseen, it seems to be a benevolent spirit bent only on helping and watching. One can write off the entire legend as mass hysteria, or the work of several overactive imaginations. But as one drives the twisty wooded drive leading up to the place, and sees at last the dark mansion sitting serenely on the hill, it is not hard to wonder if the spirit of a Colonel, long dead, might not indeed walk the floors at night, watching over his beloved Shadowwood.[6]

THE SPIRITS
OF FOREST HILL

*There are certain places in the Hoosier state where time sits
uneasily on the landscape and you get the feeling that if you
listen intently enough, you might just hear the sound of
drum beats off in the distance, and see the smoke of a camp
fire – of a people long gone – but not quite forgotten. Such
a place, where the skin of time seems to be worn thin, is a
quiet subdivision located in Merrillville.*

The town of Merrillville, Indiana, has changed a great deal
in recent years. Since its incorporation as Indiana's largest town
in 1971, Merrillville has evolved into a center of commerce and
trade. Long gone are the peaceful farm fields and pastures that
once dotted the serene countryside, to be replaced by traffic
lights and shopping malls. A drive down Broadway, through
the center of town, presents a nearly unbroken string of strip
malls, parking lots, and other evidence of suburban life.

Just one block east of Broadway, however, there lies one
residential area that seems to have escaped the onrush of
development and commercialization. Bearing the quaint title of
"Forest Hills," this subdivision of older homes exudes an
atmosphere of quiet dignity and serenity. Indeed, despite being
within a stone's throw of one of the most developed areas in
Northwest Indiana, Forest Hills has apparently remained
unchanged with the passing years.

It is an area which, though geographically small, is rich in
history and lore. The land upon which Forest Hills now quietly
stands was first settled long before Merrillville, or even
Indiana, became reality. Indeed, long before the first white
man set foot in Indiana, this area was the site of a Potawatomi
Indian encampment. It was these Native Americans who first
settled the area. It was here that generations of Indians lived,
died, and presumably were buried.

Near the center of the subdivision, there lies a small spot named Lea Circle. It is said that this was the tribal meeting ground, upon which the powwows and tribal dances were held. Driving through this sleepy subdivision today, it is easy to imagine the smoke of campfires long gone and the sound of tribal drums long stilled by time.

It was here, into this subdued atmosphere, that Bill and Karen Anderson* moved in 1954 with their young daughter, Anna. Having lived in nearby Glen Park for most of their lives, Bill and Karen were anxious to escape to the 'country' surroundings that Merrillville provided. They built a small, two-story home not far from Lea Circle and settled in to enjoy the peace of the neighborhood. Both were unaware of the history of the area and, like their neighbors, the Andersons enjoyed the rustic atmosphere of the area. What they could not have guessed at the time was that the history of the place was going to reach out to them.

The Andersons moved into their new home in September of 1954. For the first few weeks, the family kept busy with the business of moving in, but as September turned to October the last of the moving boxes were packed away and the family settled into their new home. It was only then that Mrs. Anderson began to notice the peculiar behavior of their Scottish terrier, Max. During the day Max would happily pad around the home, content to play in the shady backyard or to sleep in a sunny corner. But then as evening drew near, the dog would become more and more agitated. Frequently he would race from one end of the house to the other, seemingly chasing something, or someone, that no one else in the family could see.

Then another aspect was added to the dog's bizarre behavior. For several nights in a row Max would run through the house excitedly, then suddenly stop directly in front of the dining room picture window that looked out over the back yard and cock his head to one side as though listening for something that no one else could hear. Here he would remain, sometimes sitting motionless for an hour or more, seemingly entranced. While this odd behavior was the subject of amused speculation between Mr. and Mrs. Anderson, it was not until several weeks later that they began to suspect something strange was going on.

One cool autumn evening toward the end of October, Mrs. Anderson was sitting in the living room of her new home quietly doing her mending. Her husband, who worked at US Steel in Gary, was working the four to midnight shift and her daughter Anna had been put to bed an hour before, so Mrs. Anderson was looking forward to an evening to herself. Suddenly her peace was disturbed by two events that happened almost simultaneously.

Max, at his usual station by the back yard picture window, suddenly erupted in excited barking. Thinking that a prowler might be in the back yard, Mrs. Anderson rose to see what was causing the commotion. But before she could get to the dining room she heard another sound that caused her further alarm. From her upstairs bedroom, her daughter Anna was calling out to her. Since Anna was a child who slept well and almost never called for her mother, Karen knew that something was afoot. She turned and raced upstairs to her daughter's bedroom.

As she ran down the hall to the bedroom, her daughter's shouts became clearer, "The lights Momma! Look at the pretty lights!" Karen quickly entered the room to find her daughter out of bed and leaning up against her bedroom window overlooking the back yard. She quickly crossed the room to see what her daughter was yelling about and stopped short in bewildered amazement.

"There were several balls of light," she now recalls, "dancing around in the back yard. At first I thought they might be fireflies, but I quickly realized that they were balls of light, perhaps four or five inches in diameter. There were six or eight of them. They would land in one spot for just a second and then zoom up into the air four or five feet only to come down somewhere else in the yard. There was something rhythmic in their flight, it was almost like a kind of strange dance."

Then Mrs. Anderson noticed something even stranger about these eerie 'balls.' As they flew from place to place their color would change. "They started out bright yellow, like a full moon, but as they flew they began to change. One would turn almost orange and then another would go white. I think that one turned blue. It would have been pretty if it wasn't so strange."

Entranced, Mrs. Anderson and her daughter sat by the window for nearly ten minutes watching this eerie show. "I sat there by the window with Anna in my arms, trying to think of every possible explanation. Then it occurred to me that I should call Bill at work. I just felt like I needed to let him know."

Taking her daughter with her, Mrs. Anderson left the bedroom to make the call from a downstairs phone. While waiting for her husband to be contacted, Mrs. Anderson noticed that Max had abruptly quit barking. She put the phone down for a moment and went to the dining room picture window to find that the bouncing balls of light had disappeared as mysteriously as they had come.

When Karen finally got back to the phone and spoke with Bill, his reaction was a mixture of skepticism and amusement. While believing that his wife had seen something, Bill felt that there must be a rational explanation for the phenomena. Perhaps it was headlights from passing cars reflected from nearby Broadway. Perhaps it was just swamp gas, which in unusual cases can incandesce in the atmosphere, producing a glow. In any case, Bill was not ready to believe that his family was dealing with anything in the realm of the supernatural. Within several weeks however, he was no longer so sure.

By the first week in December, Bill and Karen had all but forgotten the strange balls of light. Christmas was approaching and both were looking forward to spending the holiday season in their new home. It was then that Bill began to experience a series of strange and unsettling nightmares.

"At the time, Bill told me that he had had a number of vivid dreams in which there was someone in the house. He did not know who it was or what they wanted, but in the dreams he felt like they were very near and that they should not be there," Karen remembers. "Sometimes, he would wake up in the middle of the night and go downstairs just to make sure that it really was a dream."

Then one night shortly before Christmas, Karen Anderson was awakened about 3:00 a.m. by her husband sitting up abruptly, and violently lunging off the side of the bed. "He sort of yelled. I thought that he was having another bad dream," she said, "so I turned on the light to see what the matter was. He was standing there by the side of the bed just shaking. He looked like he was about to collapse."

Bill explained to his wife that he had indeed had another dream in which someone was in the house. This time, however, the feeling was so strong that it immediately woke him up. Opening his eyes, he was shocked to see the figure of a tall man standing next to him looking down at him intently. Bill said that he could not pick out the man's features, but he did know that he was tall and seemed to have long dark hair. When Mrs. Anderson suggested to her husband that he might have been still dreaming, Bill insisted that this was not the case. Bill was a rational, reasonable man not prone to flights of fancy. He said that he knew what he had seen and nothing could convince him otherwise.

Now both Bill and Karen began to believe that something strange was going on in their new home. They considered talking to neighbors to see if they had similar experiences, but were afraid of being branded as "kooks" by their new friends. Karen suggested talking to their minister, but Bill again demurred, realizing how incredible their story sounded. Perhaps, Bill reasoned, if they just let things go the strange happenings might go away on their own.

Indeed, for the next several weeks things seemed to calm down for the Andersons. Bill's nightmares seemed to be less frequent and even Max seemed be a bit more relaxed. But then in mid-January of 1955, there came the most startling event yet for the Andersons. Once again Karen was awakened in the middle of the night. This time however, she realized that she was alone in bed. From the vantage point of her bedroom she could see that a light was on downstairs, so she decided to make sure that everything was all right.

"I was afraid Bill had gone through another bad dream," she recalls, "so I went downstairs to the kitchen, where the light was on." Walking into the kitchen, Karen was bewildered to find her husband down on his hands and knees looking into the heating vent that led to the furnace. "I asked him what was wrong — was there was something wrong with the furnace? He jumped when I spoke. He had not heard me come in. But then he said, "'Come here Karen, you have got to hear this.'"

Karen was now more confused than ever, but something in her husband's voice made her obey his request without question. She squatted in the corner of the kitchen and put her ear to the furnace vent. "It was singing," she says today. "Singing — of more than one voice, too. It was really kind of a chant. I could not pick out any words, but the voices rose and fell in a rhythmic pattern. I looked at Bill and said, 'My God, Bill what is happening?' And then I started to cry."

Bill held his wife to comfort her and together they sat on the floor of their kitchen and listened to the strange voices for almost an hour. "Then they just sort of faded. I can't exactly tell you what happened to them, but gradually over a period of about fifteen minutes they became less and less distinct." Finally the voices were gone altogether, replaced by the common night sounds of a suburban home.

Bill and Karen Anderson spent the rest of that night sitting in the living room discussing what to do next. By now they clearly realized that something strange was happening in their beautiful new home. Further, they decided that they must tell someone else about the things that they had been experiencing. The next morning as Bill left for work, Karen placed a call to the pastor of the church that they had been attending in Glen Park. Without explaining the need for his presence, Karen invited him to their home that evening to discuss "some problems that they were having."

Undoubtedly, their pastor came to the home that evening ready to deal with anything from marital difficulty to spiritual problems. To his credit however, he did seem ready to believe the Andersons when they told him about the events of the recent months. The clergyman talked with them at length about their experiences and while he was unable to offer any rational explanation for the phenomena they described, he was at least caring and supportive.

After they discussed the situation, the pastor asked to lead Bill and Karen in prayer. The three joined hands in the living room and asked for the blessing of God on their new home and for peace to be given to whatever spirits might dwell there. After the prayer was over the pastor took his leave, asking Bill and Karen to let him know of any more disturbances in the house. "He left that night," Karen said, "and from that moment on, we never had a bit of trouble again. It was as though this was all that needed to be done."

Since that night in early 1955, the Anderson's small home in Forest Hills has been at peace. Bill's nightmares abruptly ceased after the intervention of their pastor and even Max eventually quit his sentry duty by the dining room picture window. Indeed, their new home became the kind of warm, comfortable home that they had always dreamed of owning. In time, three more children were added to the household. They grew up in a home they loved, unmolested by the spirits that had once so disrupted the household.

Bill Anderson died in 1982. Anna, their daughter, is married and lives in nearby Crown Point. Karen Anderson now lives in an apartment in Merrillville, just a few miles from Forest Hills. Whatever it was that disturbed the peace of their home has been laid to rest. Indeed, except for the occasional retelling of the tale around the kitchen table, the events of 1954 and 1955 have passed completely from their lives. "It almost seems like a bad dream now," Karen says, "except that I lived through it. I know it was real."

> Forest Hills is an area which, though geographically small, is rich in history and lore. Long before the first white man set foot in Indiana, this area was the site of a Potawatomi Indian encampment. It was here that generations of Indians lived, died, and presumably were buried. If you drive through Forest Hills subdivision at dusk on a cool October evening, you might still get the feeling that if you listen intently enough, you might just hear the sound of drum beats off in the distance, and see the smoke of a camp fire — of a people long gone — but not quite forgotten.[7]

THINGS THAT GO BUMP
IN THE NIGHT
(Or, a Porter Poltergeist)

Lying on the coast of Lake Michigan, Porter County is one of the most tranquil and beautiful places in Indiana. Home to Indiana Dunes State Park, the communities of Chesterton, Porter, and Ogden Dunes seem to have a feeling apart from the rest of Indiana. Though, on a clear day, the skyscrapers of busy Chicago may be faintly visible across the blue waters of Lake Michigan, the pace of life in this area brings to mind the feeling of warm summer breezes and the pleasant coolness of wet sand between the toes.

The communities of Chesterton and Porter, lying next to each other on the dune-filled shoreline, are charming Victorian communities that have kept their nineteenth-century charm and grace. They are also towns steeped in history.

The town of Porter sits on land that was first occupied by an older town called Waverly. Originally a land grant from President William Henry Harrison in the early 1800s. Waverly was a thriving community until a fire destroyed it in 1884. The sole surviving building was a vintage 1850 schoolhouse which now sits abandoned on Waverly Road in Porter. The chief ghost story of the region, however, deals not with the schoolhouse but with a large brick home that lies just adjacent to it.

Carol Bratcher is the proprietor of Carol's Antiques in downtown Chesterton. Carol is a gregarious, friendly woman of indeterminate age. Outgoing and personable, Carol is a direct no-nonsense business woman with a penchant for telling it the way she sees it.

However, when Carol talks of her former home in nearby Porter, her voice becomes wistful and her eyes sparkle with odd nostalgia. Odd, because the house she is describing was the scene of strange events that stretched throughout the thirty years she, her husband and nine children lived in the home.

Carol and her husband moved into the house in 1955 with their then five children. The home was comfortable and substantial and its eleven rooms provided badly needed room for an expanding family. Made of brick, the two-story house had been constructed in stages beginning in the 1890s.

The first impression that there was something odd might be going on came when Carol, then eight months pregnant with her sixth child, was unpacking boxes of utensils in the kitchen. "It was hard to describe," Carol now says. "I had the feeling that I wasn't alone. Something was there, watching me. Not an unfriendly presence, but it was as though there was someone looking over my shoulder as I unpacked." Carol passed off the feeling and busied herself with the business of establishing her new home and making ready for the birth of her next child. It was not until after the child was born in July that she began to realize there was someone — or something else — in the home.

Carol and her husband brought their son home and settled him into his new room, a downstairs bedroom, adjacent to the kitchen. This arrangement was convenient as Carol frequently found herself getting up late and using the kitchen to prepare a bottle for the baby.

Within a few weeks of bringing her new child home, Carol began to notice an uncanny, and unpleasant occurrence as she entered the kitchen late at night. "I would hit the doorway to the kitchen," she now recalls, "and a sort of panic would come over me. It was an unreasonable fear, with no sense to it at all. All I knew was that I felt like I had to get the light on in the kitchen or I would die." Rationalizing this sensation as nothing more than the work of an overactive imagination, Carol tried to ignore the feeling. But then she began to notice something else odd.

"I would get up in the night and run to turn on the light over the buffet," she says. Then she would then enter the dimly lit kitchen and turn on the light over the sink to prepare the baby's bottle. "After the baby was put back to sleep," she recalls, "I would invariably go upstairs to check on the other children and when I got back the kitchen light would be turned off. It was an old switch where you had to turn it completely one direction for 'on' and another direction for 'off.' There was no way the switch could have slipped on or off." At first, Carol thought her husband had gotten up and turned the light off, but each time she found her husband fast asleep.

Corroboration for her feelings about the kitchen came several months later when Carol confided her experiences to a neighbor. To her shock, the neighbor did not seem surprised by the story. In fact, she told Carol about an incident that had occurred in the home years before that shed light on the strange sensations Carol was experiencing.

She told Carol that the former occupant of the residence had once shared the home with her elderly mother. At that time a small office had occupied the bedroom that was now inhabited by Carol, her husband and child. One day, the neighbor reported, the old woman, alone in the house, was sitting in the office when she felt the sudden chest pains of an impending heart attack. Stumbling out of the room, the old woman rushed through the kitchen toward the dining room phone to call for help. She made it as far as the doorway between the kitchen and dining room and collapsed. She was found dead some time later, lying in the very doorway where Carol was now experiencing her feelings of panic and dread.

While such an explanation did at least partially explain her feelings, it did nothing to slow the episodes that continued to disturb the household. In fact, with the passage of time the occurrences increased in variety and intensity.

Soon the phenomena took on a strange, almost playful quality, much of it centering around the mimicking of sounds. Like many young mothers, each afternoon Carol put her younger children down for an afternoon nap. These were times of needed rest for both mother and children. Frequently, however, Carol's reverie was disturbed by the sound of the children playfully yelling and running through the upstairs section of the house. At times the sound of this raucous behavior was so tumultuous that Carol could see a downstairs light fixture which hung from the ceiling jiggle with the reverberation.

What was so unnerving about these times was the fact that invariably Carol would run upstairs only to find her children asleep in bed. "There was simply no way they could have all gotten into bed that quick," says Carol. "It had to be something else. It was like someone just wanted to keep me running." Soon the bizarre mimicking of voices went beyond the sounds of children playing.

First, there was an unusual sound like glass beads being dropped onto a marble dresser next to Carol's bed that occurred almost every night as Carol drifted off to sleep. Then there were the times when Carol's husband, a TV repairman, came in the front door and laid his tool caddie on the floor. In those days a TV repairman's case was full of glass tubes and the caddie made a very distinctive tinkle when it was laid down. "It could be clearly heard through the whole house. First there would be the opening and shutting of the door, the plop of the caddie being dropped on to the floor, and then a high, thin tinkle from the tubes inside. It was unmistakable," Carol says. The only problem was that frequently Carol and the children would hear the sound in the mid-afternoon, only to have Howard return home a half hour later.

The most direct evidence of this manipulation of sound came when Carol received a visit from her aunt, an elderly lady who was a staunch skeptic with regard to all things supernatural. Upon her arrival, Carol mentioned the strange episodes that she and her family had been experiencing but the older lady ridiculed Carol's stories. In fact, she advised Carol not to tell the story to anyone else, for fear that she would be considered a 'little odd.'

However, one night soon after her visit began, her attitude was to change. One night about 2:00 a.m. Carol was upstairs changing her daughter Eileen's diaper. As she did so she heard the sound of voices drifting up from the downstairs living room. By now used to the voices, Carol ignored the sounds and continued the task at hand. In a moment, however, Carol was joined by her aunt, who had been awakened by the noise.

"What is that?" asked her aunt.

Carol replied imperturbably, "Go back to bed. It's nothing, believe me."

"Well, I hear it!" replied the older woman, who then went downstairs to investigate for herself.

In a few moments Carol's aunt was back upstairs looking shaken. "I know what I heard!" she declared. "Your husband was downstairs playing with those kids. I heard it plain as day; but when I peeked in the bedroom, he was fast asleep! I think this damn place is haunted!"

Unable to suppress a smirk Carol faced her aunt. "Nooooo kidding!" she smugly replied.

With the passage of time, more sounds were heard in the house. Often Carol would awaken in the night to hear the sound of music or distant conversations drifting through her home when no one was awake. Carol also began to hear frequent knocking on the inside walls of the house. "It was nearly always at night. It was like someone was playing with you—trying to get you up," Carol says. These poundings climaxed one night at about midnight when Carol's husband was out of town on business. "I woke up to hear this pounding on the wall. But this was more or less a usual occurrence, so out loud I said 'I want to get some sleep, I don't want a floor show. Do your damnedest, I don't care. I'm going to sleep.'"

In response, the knockings became louder and more insistent. Still Carol ignored them and tried in vain to sleep. "It kept on getting louder and louder," she says "until the whole house was shaking. It was like lying in the middle of a big bass drum." Finally, unable to shut out the noise, Carol rose. "OK, you win. I'm up" she said to no on in particular. Reluctantly, she went to sit in the living room. The poundings immediately began to subside and by 4:00 a.m. the house was still and Carol was back in bed.

With such weird episodes occurring on a regular basis, one might well wonder if Carol and her family were living in a state of constant fear. Such, however, does not seem to be the case. "You learn to just sort of accept things and go on," Carol says "We did not think all that much about it really."

Still, some of the occurrences were hard to overlook. For instance several months after they moved in, Carol returned home from a morning of shopping to find her husband Howard sitting on the couch nursing an injured lip. After only half sarcastically asking her to never leave him alone in the home again, Howard related that he had decided to open up the attic to see if there was room there for some storage. He brought a ladder into the upstairs hall, opened the door into the ceiling, and stuck his head and shoulders through the opening.

Howard peered into the dimly-lit attic. Suddenly, as he stood looking at the empty space, a small board flew though the air and hit him squarely on the lip. As uncanny as the experience was, odder still was the fact that the board that had so mysteriously taken flight was a piece of paneling from a downstairs bedroom that had been cut the week before and discarded. Since the attic was inaccessible except through the ceiling panel and since no one had been in the attic in the preceding week, Carol and Howard were at a loss to explain how the board could have come to be in the attic, let alone acquired the gift of spontaneous flight.

There were also more sinister signs of a presence in the house. There were the sudden fears that the Bratcher's three-year-old son developed about the "strange woman in his closet" and the cold rage that seemed to sweep over Carol as she approached the closet to investigate. And there was the story of Carol's oldest son, sitting in the living room early one morning, who was slapped smartly across the cheek by an unseen hand. "I heard the smack," Carol relates "and suddenly there was a red mark across his face."

Still, not all the manifestations were quite so threatening. In fact, much of the time the ghostly events were playful and almost childlike. Perhaps this may shed light on to the fact that the only sightings of the ghost seemed to indicate a child's presence. Carol's oldest son was the first to catch a glimpse of their spectral intruder. While upstairs one afternoon ironing a pair of jeans, he was surprised to catch a fleeting glimpse of a child rounding the corner of the hall and running toward the stairs. Thinking it was one of his younger siblings headed for a fall, the young man ran out into the hall yelling for the child to stop. No one was in the hall, or for that matter the entire upstairs level of the house.

Carol was next to see the child, also heading for the stairs. "I was downstairs in the kitchen and I saw this kid come running around the corner, going like sixty for the stairs. It was a child the size of one of mine—I would guess two or three years old. Thinking it was one of my kids, I ran over in a hurry to stop them, but when I got to the stairs there was no one there."

It was Howard who was the last to see the diminutive apparition. One night, unable to sleep, Howard sat in the living room reading. About 3:00 a.m. he was surprised to see a child peeking at him around the corner of the stairway. Thinking there was a child on the steep staircase, he quickly rose and ran to the stairway, only to find it empty. The hide-and-seek ghost had struck again.

Still, despite all of the phenomena Carol and her family experienced in their thirty years at the Porter home, they seem to have taken it much in stride. In talking about the experiences now, Carol seems almost wistful about their family poltergeist.

However, the ghostly episodes are a bit more unsettling for Mike and Diana Jones, who now live in the house. Mike and Diana moved into the home in January of 1994 after inheriting the home from Mike's father, who had purchased it from the Bratchers.

Mike relates that, prior to moving in, he had been told by his father about some of the odd occurrences in the house and he himself had even been present for a few unexplainable events. "One thing I remember distinctly," Mike now recalls, "was the time my father and I were standing in the kitchen talking when suddenly there was a sound like a semi-truck ramming the house. It shook the house. I literally thought someone had rammed the house but . . . there was no explanation. We looked everywhere, and nothing had fallen, nothing was out of place. It was strange to say the least." Despite this preview of coming events, Mike and his wife did not give much thought to moving into a haunted house as they unloaded their furniture that cold winter day. However, in the weeks to come, the Jones' began to think about it a great deal.

The first person to have contact with whatever inhabits the home was the Jones' two-year-old son. Shortly after moving into their new home, their son began to claim to be afraid of going upstairs to his bedroom at night. When questioned as to why he was afraid, the boy replied, "Because of Frieda. She is the lady in my closet. She scares me."

Ordinarily such a response might be passed off as nothing more than the product of childhood imagination. What the Jones' could not know was that this was the same closet in which Carol Bratcher's son claimed to have seen a 'scary woman' years earlier.

This was not their son's last brush with the ghost. One day in 1996 their son was descending the stairs from his bedroom toward Diana, who was waiting for him on the landing below. Two or three steps from the bottom, the boy smiled to his mother and suddenly jumped the remaining steps into her arms.

Seeing the danger in such a maneuver, Diana upbraided her son. "That's dangerous," she cautioned, "Please don't do that again!"

Wide-eyed, the boy replied "But I do it all the time with the shadow." Sensing something strange, Diana asked her son, "Who is the shadow?"

"He is in my room and on the stairs," the child replied. Now joining the conversation, Mike asked, "How big is the shadow?"

"About this big" said the child, indicating a height about four feet from the ground. "That tall?" asked Mike. "Well, not really," said the boy, "he is floating, and so his feet are not on the ground."

Though certainly startling this was not to be the only experience the Jones' were to have with their unseen guest. Frequently they have heard the sound of doors slamming in the home despite the fact that later examination revealed all the doors to be shut and securely locked. Other incidents involved objects being suddenly misplaced. "You can take a can of pop out of the refrigerator, put it down, turn you back for a moment and it will be gone, with no one else in the house. Later it will turn up in some odd place where you would never expect it to be," comments Mike.

Stranger still was the experience Mike and Diana shared several months later as they went to bed for the night. Diana, who cannot see well without the aid of glasses, handed them to her husband, who carefully placed them on a night stand next to their bed. Then, turning off the lights, they went to sleep, only to be awakened in the middle of the night to find the light switch in their room had mysteriously been turned on and the overhead light was now shining directly in their faces. In their effort to extricate themselves from bed to investigate, Diana asked Mike for her glasses but they were not to be found on the bed stand where he had laid them just hours earlier. Instead, they were discovered neatly folded, lying between them. "It may sound silly," Mike says, "but that light turned itself on and those glasses were not where I had put them. I know that much for a fact."

Whatever is causing the disturbances has also not lost its talent for reproducing common sounds. Mike reports that several times, while getting ready for work early in the morning, he has heard the sound of his children playing upstairs in their room, only to investigate and find them asleep. Diana reports that sitting in the family room one early morning she was startled to hear a child's voice greeting her with a cheery "Hi!" that came, seemingly, out of thin air.

Both Mike and Diana have felt cold spots in the house as well. Mike tells of walking though a cold spot on the stairs that "made the hairs on my arms stand straight up." Significantly, although neither Mike or Diana have spoken with Carol Bratcher about her experiences in the house, both have reported a cold spot in the kitchen doorway . . . exactly where Carol felt her sense of panic.

The haunting events did not limit themselves to the human inhabitants of the house. The Jones' two dogs seem to sense something amiss in the home as well. At times, both dogs have refused to enter the small bedroom off the kitchen. Once, after being shut in the room for an afternoon, one normally docile dog was found burrowed under some packing boxes, panting in fear. Examination revealed a patch of fur had been torn from her side. "The size was as though someone had taken their two hands together and grabbed her fur and just yanked," comments Mike.

In the winter of 1996 the manifestations increased in their severity. Both Mike and Diana began to notice a foul odor accompanied by a cold spot that seemed to move around the house. First it was noticed in an upstairs bedroom, and then later, on the stair landing. At this point both Mike and Diana noted that the door slamming became more frequent and louder.

The most dramatic event, however, occurred one day in January when Diana was visited both by her mother and by one of her close friends who had brought along her young son. As the women sat chatting and drinking coffee in the living room, the boys played noisily around them. After a while Diana suggested that the boys go to her son's room and play and the boys happily went upstairs. After a moment, however, Diana's son returned and announced "I can't get the door to my room open!" Puzzled, Diana replied, "Well, it shouldn't be stuck. Let's go find out."

The women went upstairs to try their luck at opening the door but although the doorknob moved, the door itself would not budge. Putting her full weight against the door, Diana felt something move slightly on the other side. With repeated effort, she was able to open the door far enough to stick her head in and saw that a large wooden dresser had been pushed in front of the door!

"That was crazy," says Mike. "The door opens in, and the only way out is through a second-story window. Even if my son had tried to move that dresser, he could not. It weighs a ton."

Since that time, the manifestations have calmed somewhat. Both Diana and Mike still report the occasional odd sound or strange happening. Recently, Mike was alone in the home when he heard an upstairs door open, footsteps proceed down the hall, and a bedroom door slam. Predictably, investigation revealed he was alone in the house.

Despite these occurrences, by-and-large the manifestations seem to have eased, at least for the moment. No one can guess how or when they will return. Still, the Jones', like the Bratchers before them, seem to take the situation in stride. "It is sure strange sometimes," says Mike, "but I guess you live with it."

Perhaps though, it is the inimitable Carol Bratcher who puts it best. "A lot of people don't want to talk about things like this," she says, "but I figure, you take whatever nature throws your way, and I don't see any point in sitting and worrying about it." Perhaps she has a point.

Sitting in the quiet town of Porter, nestled close to the beauty of the Indiana dunes, lies a large Victorian house. It looks, from the outside, like many homes of its kind. On the inside, however, two families believe that something inexplicable lurks. Something at times playful and at times darkly forbidding. Something that walks the floors at night slamming doors and begging to be noticed. Perhaps, as Carol Bratcher holds, it is a poltergeist, or noisy ghost.

Perhaps it is the spirit of a child that has been glimpsed by residents of the home. Perhaps no one will ever know. However, one thing that is known is that somewhere in the quaint town of Porter, there lies a classically haunted house fresh from the annals of Indiana ghost lore.[8]

PART IV

BRIDGES OF DOOM, TUNNELS INTO DARKNESS, AND HIGHWAYS TO THE HEREAFTER

The Vanishing Hitchhiker
of Reeder Road

The Legend of
White Lick Creek Bridge

The Ghosts of Cline Avenue

The history of Indiana is tied, in large part, to the history of transportation. Beginning with the first white settlers passing through Indiana's fields and hills in Conestoga wagons, searching for the wide open spaces of the midwest to the rail system that followed, Indiana has always served as a collection point for travelers moving on in search of greener pastures. Today, Indiana has become a hub of transportation. A quick glance at a current map of Indiana reveals an intricate highway and railway system all dedicated to fulfilling the American need to get from point A to point B as quickly as possible.

Interestingly, our transportation system has become a part of Indiana ghost lore as well. Brown County has a long-held tale that one of its famous covered bridges is haunted by a ghostly buggy which can be seen entering one side of the bridge, never to reappear out the other end. Highway 37, which stretches from Indianapolis to Bloomington, is said to be haunted by a ghostly sedan from the 1930s, which crashed and burned while carrying several students to Indiana University some sixty years ago.

Some of these legends are benign and almost charming in their own way. Others, however, are of a darker, more ominous nature. Although separate from one another in miles and history, all tell stories of tragedy, horror, and a longing for some final resolution that goes beyond death itself.

While the images of a haunted bridge or road may not seem as romantic as the classic picture of a dark rambling mansion, they are nonetheless part of Indiana's ghostly traditions. And if you should find yourself traveling down a Hoosier road one dark night, with the fog hugging the ground and clouds passing over the moon, you might well pause to wonder — who knows where any road really leads?

THE VANISHING HITCHHIKER OF REEDER ROAD

It is an old story of course. Tales of her have been passed down through time from throughout the globe. The 'vanishing hitchhiker' as she is popularly known, has been with us since the dawn of transportation. The first legend of her appearance has been traced back over 800 years to Ancient China, where she was said to have petitioned a ride from a temple priest traveling by night in a rickshaw.

Indiana, of course, can boast of its own encounters with the celebrated vanishing hitchhiker. During the 1930s, two WPA workers, driving by night toward a meeting in Indianapolis, claimed to have met a strange young woman who begged a ride with them, only to vanish mysteriously as they sped through the small town of Fishers. Other reports have her being picked up by college students on their way back to Bloomington after Christmas vacation, and one variant from the late nineteenth century even tells of her pleading for transportation from a horse-and-buggy traveling through Brown County. Perhaps the most classic retelling of this tale, however, centers on a barren expanse of road in Northwest Indiana named "Reeder Road" by the local inhabitants.

Stretching for about eight miles between Merrillville and neighboring Griffith, Reeder Road is as desolate and foreboding a piece of roadway as one might find in the Hoosier State. It is a thoroughfare surrounded on all sides by dark woods and swamps, broken only by the occasional junk yard, and, sadly, the inevitable refuse that can be found on back roads all across America.

By day, travelers down Reeder Road might only note the desolate geography of the area, but at night the roadway seems to take on a more ominous character. In point of fact, a traveler down this route in the dark might well be justified in such an impression because as late as the early 1980s, the headless body of a man was found deposited in the swampy woods adjacent to Reeder Road.

Reeder Road
Photograph by Kris Harrison

However, the chief ghost story associated with Reeder Road does not deal with this unlucky individual, but centers instead around a mysterious young woman who is said to frequent the road late at night and one unlucky youth who had a disconcerting experience with her.

It was late on a rainy spring night when Randy* turned his car off Nicholson Road onto Reeder Road. It was later, perhaps, than he cared for it to be. A senior at Griffith High School, he had gone to Merrillville on a Friday night date. After taking his girlfriend to a movie, Randy had taken his date home and could not resist her invitation to "come in for a few minutes . . ."

Now the clock on his dashboard read almost 11:30 p.m., which allowed him barely enough time to get home before his midnight curfew. He found himself accelerating slightly as he thought of his parents' anger if he were to come in late yet again.

It was the early 1970s, and the radio in his car blared "Billy don't be a hero," and other eminently forgettable Top Forty hits offered up by WLS in Chicago. The sound of the music seemed to keep beat with the click of the windshield wipers as he drove through the darkness. A soft drizzle had started and in his hurry Randy reminded himself to keep his speed under control. The only thing worse than his parents' wrath at a violation of his curfew was the prospect of explaining a dent in the fender from sliding into a tree.

So intent was Randy on avoiding his parent's displeasure that he was almost upon the girl before he saw her. Through the splatters of rain on the windshield she suddenly appeared just off the roadway, her arm raised in supplication, a look of near desperation on her face. Instinctively, Randy veered his car to the left to avoid the figure, and then almost before he realized it, he was braking his car to a stop on the shoulder of the road.

In a moment her face appeared at his side window and before he could react she was opening the rear door and gliding silently into the back seat. Randy would later recall that it seemed strange that she chose the back seat rather than sitting next to him in the front, but at the moment all he could do is stare at his new companion.

"Thanks for stopping," the girl said in a whisper that somehow cut through the noise of the vehicle. "My car went off the road and I have been waiting a long time to get a ride home." For a moment Randy was unsure of just what to say. His thoughts quickly flashed to home, his parents, and his curfew, but with a glance back at the helpless girl he quickly decided his parents would understand his being a Good Samaritan.

"I didn't see any car along the road," Randy replied. "Where is it? Maybe we can just pull you out."

"Just take me home," the girl replied, a smile quickly passing across her face. "It would be easier that way."

The girl directed Randy to reverse his direction and drive toward a rustic section of Calumet township called Ross. Randy knew the area well enough to recognize her directions as passing by the old Ross Cemetery, past the nearby school, and onto a side road.

"You can't miss the house," she said. "It has white clapboard shingles, and a porch out front. I'm sure the light will be on — my parents must be worried sick."

Randy stole another look at the young girl and was able to see her clearly for the first time. What he saw made his breath catch in his throat for a moment. The lights from the dashboard somehow seemed to reflect back on her as she sat hunched in the seat, bathing her in a cool even glow. Indeed, she seemed almost luminescent as she stared absently out the window at the rain.

She was young, not more than seventeen, Randy decided, with flowing blond hair that streamed down her face due to her damp condition. Indeed, she seemed drenched to the skin. Her hair hung in rivulets down almost to her large, dark eyes. Her dress, as damp and soiled as the rest of her, looked formal, as though she had been at a dance or dinner that evening. In passing, Randy thought she must be poor, as her dress seemed oddly out-of-date. Despite her condition, however, Randy could not help but note that she was oddly attractive, and this pushed thoughts of his parents and curfew further from his mind.

As they drove on through the misty night, Randy tried to make conversation with the girl but without success. After giving directions to her home she settled back into a dreamy silence, punctuated only with an occasional grunt of affirmation at something he said. The only time she was roused from her stupor was when, noting that she must be cold, Randy offered her his Griffith High School letterman's jacket, which was lying next to him on the seat.

"Yes," she said wearily. "I'd be grateful. It feels like I have been cold forever, and I'd like to get warm."

Without further comment Randy handed the coat back to the girl, who put it around her shoulders and then sank back into her silent reflection. Thinking to himself that there was something a bit odd about this attractive stranger, Randy returned his eyes to the road as he maneuvered the last turn onto Ross. Ahead in the mist, Randy could make out the tall iron fence that surrounded the old Ross Cemetery. Beyond the fence, he could just make out the shapes of a few old tombstones reflected in his headlights, a dull gray against the inky blackness of the night.

In a moment he passed Ross School, and ahead lay the hill that bore his turnoff. Unsure, now, of his directions, Randy glanced quickly once again in the direction of his back seat. "Is this the road, off here to the left? I think I remember . . ." Randy never completed his sentence.

She was gone.

Without thinking Randy slammed the brakes hard, wrestling his car onto the shoulder of the road. The car bumped, slid in the gravel for a second, and then stopped. Randy jumped out of the car, leaving the door open in his haste. He ran to the rear passengers door and opened it wide, searching for some sign of his mysterious guest, but to no avail. The harsh illumination from the dome light showed the back seat to be totally and inexorably vacant.

Shocked almost beyond belief, Randy stood in the early spring rain for nearly five minutes looking at the back seat. Clearly, rational explanations were impossible. If the girl had opened the door to make a hasty exit, he would have known it—the dome light of his car would have alerted him immediately. The window next to the seat was rolled up against the rain and even if it had been down, it would be difficult for the girl to squeeze out. More importantly, it seemed unlikely that the girl would have jumped from the vehicle. She had seemed calm, almost tranquil when he had spoken to her—not the type of girl who would make a sudden, perhaps suicidal, jump from a car going forty-five miles an hour.

As Randy stood in the rain that evening he tried to find a logical explanation for what had happened, but it evaded him. For a moment he thought he might have dreamed the event but as he placed his hand on the car seat, he felt a cold, moist spot where the girl had been.

Still, by the time morning came, Randy had managed to convince himself that the entire event might have indeed been some sort of hallucination. When he had arrived home the night before, fully an hour after his curfew, his expectation of his parent's anger was realized. Even when he haltingly explained that he had stopped to help a girl whose car had run off the road, his parents were skeptical, particularly since Randy became agitated and evasive when pressed for details. Still, something in his demeanor had made his parents believe that something odd had happened that night. They had told him to go to bed and that his punishment would be discussed the next day.

Perhaps it was to avoid just such a discussion that Randy got up early the next morning and headed toward the door. He had not slept well the night before, but now the light of day seemed to bring reason and order back to the world. Perhaps, Randy thought, it had all been a strange dream after all. Maybe he had, in fact, fallen asleep at the wheel and dreamed the entire event. In any case, he was more than willing to forget the events of the night before, and get back to the sanity of "real life."

But his coat was gone.

It was not on the coat hook in the entrance hall, where he normally would have put it when coming in the night before. It was not in the piles of clothing that surrounded his bed. It was only when he went to look for it in his car that the reality of the events of the night before came back to him. Whoever his mysterious guest had been, and however unaccountable her departure from his car, she had taken his new letterman coat with her. With fear in his heart, he quickly scanned the morning paper for news of a girl's body found along the roadway in Ross, but gratefully found nothing.

Finally, not knowing quite what else to do, he decided to retrace his path of the night before. Maybe retracing the events in the light of day would help make some sense of them. However, as he slowly drove his vehicle down Whitcomb Avenue toward Ross, the entire event seemed no less mysterious. As he passed Ross Cemetery and Ross School, he finally found his car climbing the hill toward the turnoff to the house the girl had described. He slowed for a moment, noted the patch of gravel where his car had stopped the night before, and then, almost on a whim, turned his car down the small road that the girl had described.

Any thought that the events of the night before had been a dream vanished when, about a half mile down the road, Randy saw a small home appear along the road before him. It was old and obviously unmaintained. The morning sun shone down on peeling white clapboard shingles, and the front porch tilted at a crazy angle. His heart beating hard in his chest, Randy pulled into the weed-strewn gravel driveway and slowly got out of his car.

Clearly, he had no idea what to do next. The house looked abandoned, but even if someone were to come to the door, he did not know how to begin to explain about the girl he had encountered the previous evening, her description of this house as her home, and the mysterious events of the night before.

While Randy stood reflecting on his dilemma, he was barely conscious of a car in the road behind him coming to a slow stop. A window was rolled down and an weathered voice called out "You looking for someone here, son?"

Randy turned and saw an elderly man at the wheel of a red pickup truck. The man was scrutinizing Randy closely as he said, "I'm Mr. Weaver, from down the road. Are you lost?"

"No," Randy replied, "I mean, I don't think so . . . I mean, I think I'm looking for someone who lives here."

"Well, no one lives here," the man replied sharply. "Nobody has lived here for fifteen years."

Now totally dumbfounded, Randy replied, "But I just met someone . . . last night, who gave me directions to this house. She said she lived here and . . ."

"Well, if someone told you that, they were just lying, that's all," chirped the elderly gentleman. "There ain't been nobody here for a long time. I ought to know—I've lived down the road all my life. Wilsons used to live here, but they moved away more than fifteen years ago, after their daughter died. Moved out east, to Boston I think. Mrs. Wilson had some family there, and . . ."

"A daughter?" Randy queried.

"Yes, Elizabeth was her name. Beautiful thing too. Such a shame. She died about seventeen years ago. Went to a dance in Griffith, and was driving back when her date lost control and drove off the road into a swamp. She was knocked unconscious and thrown from the car. They found her the next day, face down in the swamp. She was not in but a foot of water, but she had drowned on account of her being knocked out by the wreck."

Suddenly Randy's mind reeled. "Killed? Are you sure?" The man frowned and looked at Randy closer than before. "Of course I'm sure. I went to the funeral. She's buried out at Ross Cemetery, not two miles from here. Lovely young thing. Sure a tragedy. Killed by a hot-rodding boyfriend on one of those back roads."

"Which road?" asked Randy, thinking perhaps that he did not really want an answer.

"Why it was Reeder Road," came the reply. "Just outside of Griffith as it went through the woods."

Ten minutes later, Randy, still shaking from his interview with the old man, got into his car and slowly drove back toward the main road. His mind reeling, he turned south to make his way home. As he passed Ross School he saw the old cemetery gates appear in the distance.

Randy now says he does not know exactly what it was that made him pull up to the gates of Ross Cemetery. Perhaps it was disbelief about all that had happened in the last twenty-four hours. Perhaps it was some sort of morbid curiosity. Whatever the reason, Randy pulled into the small drive that wound its way through the cemetery. Walking the rows of the cemetery, he noted tombstones dating back to the early part of the last century. After fifteen minutes of aimless wandering, he gave up finding what he had come to look for. As he turned to make his way to his car, a wave of relief swept through him. Perhaps, he thought, he had not wanted to find her tombstone after all.

It was only then that something caught his eye. A flash of color among the gravestones. Something that should not have been there.

The headstone stood in a quiet corner, apart from the other graves and looked much newer. It was a small stone marked simply, "Elizabeth," and with dates beneath. If Randy had been looking, he might have noticed that the second date was the same as the night that he had picked up the beautiful young hitchhiker.

But Randy was not looking at the dates. He was not looking at the name, or even the headstone itself. He was looking with glazed horror at something that lay before the tombstone. An object that stopped his heart in his chest, and would haunt his sleep for many years to come.

A letterman's jacket, folded neatly and laying on the gently rounded mound of the grave.

It is an old story, of course. Reports of the vanishing hitchhiker have filtered down through the ages and some argue that they are really nothing more than an urban legend. But if you are driving on a misty spring evening down a barren stretch of road in northwest Indiana called Reeder Road, it might be best to keep your eyes on the road and your foot on the gas pedal. For who knows but that you might see the plaintive form of a young girl, trying in vain to find a home that she left more than forty years ago to enter into the annals of Indiana ghost lore.[9]

THE LEGEND OF
WHITE LICK CREEK BRIDGE

"Do not go gentle into that good night . . ."
Dylan Thomas

Dad Jones stood on the trestle, the sweat glistening on his skin in the hot sun. As the wet cement began to pour into the pylon, suddenly the supporting scaffolding collapsed and he plunged headlong into a sea of wet cement. Cement continued to cascade down on him, forever sealing him into the bridge – and into the annals of Indiana ghost lore.

This disquieting tale deals with a railroad bridge a few miles distant from Avon, Indiana, just east of Indianapolis. A daylight drive down a quiet country road to view the bridge reveals only a crumbling railroad trestle that once held the tracks for the Indiana Inter-Urban Railway. In the heat of a summer day, water from the creek below condenses on the concrete pylons supporting the bridge and runs down to the water below, staining the concrete with a reddish-brown hue. The sunlight from above does not permeate the interior skeleton of the bridge, leaving dark shadows beneath the superstructure.

By the light of a full moon however, the scene looks very different. The surrounding fields are bathed in a luminescent glow and wisps of mist rise from the ground below to grip the land like a shroud. The bridge itself lies still and quiet, yet somehow forbidding, like a slumbering giant, waiting to be awakened. It is on nights such as these that he is said to return. Return, to scream and rage at the injustice done him—an injustice that robbed him of his eternal rest and doomed him to be eternally imprisoned in the cold grip of the bridge itself.

There are several tales told of the man who is said to haunt the bridge. The most colorful tale, however, centers around a figure called Dad Jones. A figure that was said to be larger than life during his day and, if the tale is to be believed, may well have been larger than death itself.

It was in the first years of this century that the White Lick Creek Bridge was constructed. America was rapidly expanding and flexing its considerable financial might. A railway was needed to link the industrial center of Chicago with the burgeoning commercial settlements of the midwest. Construction of transportation systems was at an all-time high nationally and it became clear that it was necessary to connect Indianapolis with Terre Haute so goods and passengers could embark for points west. During the spring and summer of 1907 the Inter-Urban Railroad Commission was busy building just such a economic lifeline in the form of a new railway.

Through the snows of late winter and the rains of early spring the railway slowly pushed its way south and west. Most of the hard and often dangerous work of building trestles and laying the track was not done by permanent railroad employees. Instead, for these jobs the railroad opted to hire short-term workers from the surrounding areas, often field hands from local farms. Once the spring crops were planted there was a steady supply of cheap labor — farm workers who were willing to spend two or three weeks of backbreaking labor for the extra money it afforded.

In late August, however, progress was abruptly halted. It was now high summer in Indiana and time for the hay to be mown and the harvest to be brought in. Farmers and hired hands abandoned their temporary railway work to return to the fields. Almost overnight, railroad officials were disheartened to see their labor supply wither to a handful of permanent workers and supervisors. Clearly something had to be done. A new source of cheap labor must be found if the construction schedule was to be maintained.

Word was sent to railroad offices in Gary, Chicago, and Cincinnati. Postings were made in the cities offering any able-bodied man a chance for gainful employment. Soon, trains full of young and old men were moving toward central Indiana. Some came from the poorest segments of city life. Others were immigrants, new to the country and eager for a job of any kind. All were ready to grasp the opportunity given them by the railway.

The work was begun again. Indeed the new workmen were quick to make up the lost time. Rapidly becoming acclimated to long hours of backbreaking work, these men powered the railway construction as it moved forward toward Indianapolis. Railway officials were delighted. Not only was the labor cheap and the workmen tireless, but because few, if any, of the workmen were permanent railway employees, the question of the their safety was a secondary consideration.

It was only matter of time, then, until tragedy struck. It occurred in the swampy woods outside of Avon, Indiana, just a few miles from Indianapolis, as the workmen labored to build a concrete bridge over White Lick Creek. Wooden forms were built for the supporting pylons and cement was brought in by special rail car to be poured into them to make the columns. On the very first day of the concrete work, however, an accident occurred that would forever seal the fate of the bridge and would indelibly ensure this bridge its place in Indiana ghost lore.

It was a hot August morning as the itinerant workmen mixed the cement for the first pylon. After the right mixture of cement and water was reached, the cement was poured into a huge bucket and then raised by winch to the workmen above who waited to discharge the cement into the wooden frame of the pylon.

Standing on the platform above was a huge black man known to his co-workers as Dad Jones. Fully 6'5" in height, with an intimidating physique and a surly disposition, Dad Jones was known and feared by workmen and supervisors alike. It was said that he was the strongest man on the crew — he could lift more and work longer than any man on the railroad. Yet by nature he was sullen and irritable. Perhaps because of his surly nature, perhaps due the working conditions or perhaps since he was one of the few black men working on the crew, he was often given the most grueling and dangerous work. Whatever the case, Dad Jones was known as a man to be respected from a distance.

By mid-morning Dad Jones, stripped to the waist with the sweat already glistening off of his rippling muscles, stood waiting impatiently for the second load of concrete to be lifted to him and his crew. When it came, Jones and a fellow worker grappled the heavy load and maneuvered it over the form. Once this was accomplished, they tipped the bucket and the cement began to flow into the hole below.

It happened, they say, before anyone could react. The wooden platform upon which Dad Jones and the other laborer stood suddenly gave way. One worker was thrown from the platform to the ground below, but with a hoarse scream Dad Jones fell headlong into a sea of wet cement. He struggled for a moment, beating his fist against the wooden forms, but as the remaining cement cascaded down onto the form of the hapless black man, his screams stopped and he was sealed into the pylon forever.

From the perspective of the railroad foreman there was not much that could be done. Even if the body could have been recovered, he was unwilling to stop construction and tear apart a cement pylon to find the body of a black workman. Some of the more superstitious workmen protested, saying that the spirit of the workman could not rest if he was denied a proper Christian burial, but the supervisors scoffed at the suggestion.

Instead, after a delay of two hours, during which railroad officials conferred by telegraph, construction was continued. The platform over the cement pillar was rebuilt and more cement was poured into the molds, forever entombing the body of Dad Jones.

In less than two weeks the bridge was complete and the railroad moved on toward Indianapolis. Eventually, the section of railway between Indianapolis and Danville was completed and the temporary workmen were sent home. Except in the vague memories of a few railroad workers, the story of Dad Jones was quietly forgotten.

Then the screaming began.

It was first reported by a local farmer. Trekking back through the fields one moonlit night after an evening of raccoon hunting, the man found himself beneath the White Lick Creek Bridge just as an engine of the New York Central, bearing freight for Indianapolis, crossed over the expanse. Just before the train crossed the first trestle, the man swore that he heard, over the sound of the locomotive, a man's cry piercing the night. It seemed to come, he said, not from the train tracks above, but from within the bridge itself.

Naturally, this report was met with some skepticism by the local populace. Within a month, however, a similar story was reported, this time by local teenagers. They reportedly said that late one night they were walking along the tracks toward town, coming back from visiting a friend in an outlying neighboring. Though they had walked the path many times, they were nervous walking the rails that night, particularly over the bridge, where they could not escape if a train approached. Indeed, they were almost across the bridge when they heard the warning whistle of an approaching train and running the last few yards, they darted off the bridge and into the underbrush to await its passing.

Just as the train approached the opposite side of the bridge, the teenagers heard a man's guttural scream emanate from the underside of the trestle. Though the sound of the passing locomotive was thunderous in their ears, it could not mask the anguished sound that somehow seemed to cut through the noise around them. Immediately after the train passed, the screaming abruptly stopped, only to be replaced with a dull thumping sound as though something, or someone, was hammering their fist against the concrete supporting columns below.

Now completely unnerved, the boys ran the remaining distance to Avon and awakened the local sheriff. Explaining that something was wrong out at the railroad bridge and thinking that someone might be hurt, they asked the sheriff to investigate. Doubtful of the boys' story and none too pleased to be awakened from sleep, the sheriff loaded the boys into his car and drove them back to the bridge. Except for the chirp of the crickets and the croaking of frogs, all was quiet. The sheriff shone a lantern around the bridge, and seeing no one, took the boys home.

The next morning, telling the story to some of his cronies at a local store, the sheriff wrote the incident off to boys sampling some "liquid courage " or just the overactive imagination of adolescence. What was to happen next, however, even he could not ignore.

This time it was a train engineer whose engine was pulling a single flatcar west from Indianapolis. It was late June and the engineer was winding his way from Indianapolis to Danville to pick up a load bound for St. Louis. As he approached the bridge over White Lick Creek Creek, he saw something that caused him to slow his engine. It was a mist that seemed to float up from the chasm below the bridge onto the double track, taking almost human form. For a moment it held its form and then just as quickly it dissipated.

Unsure of what it was that he had just seen, the engineer slowed his train to a crawl. Then, just as he approached the bridge itself, another sight momentarily stopped his heart. "It was," he later reported, "as though the track over the first pylon was gone. I could see it clearly in the headlight—a gaping hole where the track should have been. A deep hole that seemed to go down into the center of the pylon itself. Like a part of the supporting column had just disappeared."

Thinking that part of the bridge had inexplicably collapsed, the engineer pulled hard on his emergency break. The train bucked and then slowed to a stop at the foot of the bridge. Grabbing a lantern, the engineer jumped out to investigate the damage but, unaccountably, by the time he climbed out of his engine the vision was gone. Under the light of the train headlight he could see that the tracks were there, straight and true over the length of the expanse. Now totally dumbfounded, the engineer walked the length of the bridge and then slowly retraced his steps toward the locomotive.

As he passed the first pylon, he was further disconcerted to hear a dull thumping sound emanating from beneath the bridge. A dull thumping sound such as a man might make striking concrete with his fist. The man peered carefully over the bridge to see if anyone were at the bottom of the structure but below he only saw darkness and mist. He called into the night but the continued rhythmic pounding was the only sound he heard in reply.

Losing no time in returning to the safety of his locomotive, the engineer released the emergency brake and the engine slowly inched its way over the bridge. He was almost over it when he heard the final element to this haunting vignette. A low, gruff moan swept over the bridge, like a man in his dying moments. Without looking back, the engineer pushed his throttle forward and the train sped through the night toward Danville.

Much to his credit, the engineer did not keep silent about his experience. On reaching Danville, he telegraphed his main office to ask for an inspection of the bridge, adding that "railroad safety" might well be at stake. By the next morning, a team of inspectors arrived in Avon and word of the conductor's experience swept through the town like a contagion. That afternoon, accompanied by most of the town's population, the inspectors walked the mile or so out to the bridge, and carefully examined every inch of the structure. Nothing appeared to be wrong.

It was only then that one of the townspeople pointed out a strange detail. Water, evaporating from the stream below was condensing on the bottom of the bridge and streaming in small rivulets down its sides. Such was to be expected in the heat of a summer afternoon. However, in this case the water seemed to be a brownish-red color, staining the side of the structure the hue of blood.

The railroad inspectors scoffed at the observation, explaining the uncommon color as mineral residue from the creek below. Making their evaluation, they left the area quickly and there the matter stood. Still, stories began to circulate that the dead workman had returned—that he could not rest because of the burial denied him.

Through the years, tales have been told in the surrounding region about the haunted bridge and the ill-fated workman's return. Through the generations, the locale has become a popular gathering spot for the young of the area and some have reported alleged encounters with the ghost. Some are said to have seen strange shapes in the mist at night but most reports center around hearing a low, muffled scream coming from the interior of the bridge, just as a train is about to pass over.

To this day the legend persists that, if you wait patiently by the foot of the bridge on a night of the full moon, you will be rewarded by seeing the specter of the dead workman rise from his stone tomb and shake his fist as a train passes, screaming in an unearthly voice. Believers also point out the stains that periodically reappear on the bridge on hot summer afternoons. Rivulets of water streaming down the support columns of the bridge, staining it the color of blood.

Logical explanations for most of these phenomena have, of course, been offered. Many have sought to write off the tales told as mere small town nonsense, with no basis in fact. However, in the area of Avon the stories endure. At least some of the good townspeople, if asked, will show scorn for those who seek to dismiss the ghost of White Lick Creek Bridge as fable. Others will, if you have the time, tell you the story of the doomed workman, sealed forever in concrete, destined to haunt the bridge, eternally crying out against his fate.

The image of a haunted bridge may not seem as romantic as the classic image of a dark, rambling mansion, but it is nonetheless part of Indiana's ghostly traditions. Stories of tragedy, horror, and a longing for some final resolution that goes beyond death itself — as in this tale of the White Lick Creek Bridge whose cold grip may harbor the spirit of a doomed worker forever encased in concrete and fated to eternal and unquiet unrest.[10]

THE GHOSTS OF
CLINE AVENUE

Northwest Indiana is an area unto itself. A sprawling, industrialized complex, there seems little room here for whim or fancy. Yet even in this urban setting ghost lore abounds. Especially, on one well-traveled road called Cline Avenue, the legends persist of two women whose lives, and deaths, are bound together in tragedy. Two female specters tied to the area by their fate and known as the Cline Avenue Ghosts.

Northwest Indiana is geographically located within the confines of the Hoosier state but the Calumet Region, as it is known, bears little resemblance to the rest of the state. Stretching north and west along the Lake Michigan shoreline from Gary to the Illinois border, a tour of the area reveals a thick encrustation of industry of all kinds. Smokestacks and mammoth factories seem to erupt from the very earth, creating a surreal landscape unlike any other in Indiana. Indeed, the huge manufacturing plants and rusting oil refineries stand in stark contrast to the corn fields and small towns that make up much of the rest of Indiana.

The development of northwest Indiana as a major industrial center began in 1906 when US Steel built its first facility in Gary. With Lake Michigan providing easy transportation for raw material and finished goods, it was an ideal place for industry. Soon, US Steel was joined by Bethlehem Steel and a host of other heavy industry began to develop. Immigrants from across the country and around the world flocked to the area to pursue the American dream.

Over the years, the fortunes of northwest Indiana have risen and fallen with the fate of heavy industry. Today, many of the factories and refineries that once provided goods for the nation lie abandoned and quiet. Railroad cars once used to transport steel to the docks of Whiting and Hammond stand rusting and unused on dusty railroad spurs. The golden age of the region seems to have faded into history. Still, manufacturing does continue in the large furnaces of US Steel and other factories and although industries have come and, in some cases, gone, each has left its mark on the cultural and economic life of the area.

It was industry that formed the substance of life for northwest Indiana and helped form a unique breed of people. Native "region rats," as they sometime call themselves, are direct no-nonsense people. The grit that fills the air from the smokestacks of Gary seems to have worked its way down into the native soul, producing a practical, determined group of individuals.

Little prone to romance or fancy, the Calumet region and its people bear little of the colloquial gentility characteristic of the rest of the state. It is an area well used to dealing with the realties of life and there is little space among the blast furnaces and oil storage tanks for whimsy or caprice. The wind carries with it a reminder of the nature of the region and the glowing lights on the horizon are not the romantic Northern Lights, but instead the reflection from the blast furnaces.

In such a setting, folklore and ghost legends might seem out of place. However, tales of ghosts and specters abound. For many years, US Steel employees have whispered about the infamous "Phantom of the Open Hearth," a ghostly form that is said to appear in the smoke and steam when the molten steel is poured. It is said to be that of a worker who, years before, fell into a vat of red hot liquid steel as it was being poured and who returns to haunt the spot of his demise.

Gary has the unique distinction of sporting not one but two 'clergy ghosts.' A graveyard in the old Tolleston section of Gary is said to be frequented by the ghost of a German Lutheran pastor who returns to watch over his church and flock. The Froebel section of Gary bears the strange story of a haunted light post beside Froebel School. The legend tells of a young priest from the Froebel parish who was brutally murdered while standing by the light one evening. Thereafter the street light flickered repeatedly each night at about the same hour as the priest's death. Though the bulbs were changed several times and the entire light was rewired by power company workmen, the light continued its strange memorial to the priest's death until its removal several years ago.

But far and away, however, the two chief ghosts of the area seem to be two female specters that, according to legend, haunt the same stretch of Cline Avenue between Gary and Whiting. Appropriately called the "Cline Avenue Ghosts," they have been the subject of much inquiry, speculation, and debate in past years. Some point to the cultural history of the area to explain at least one of the ghost stories. Other researchers insist that there are not two, but one, ghost. However, the oldest stories available from the area point to two distinct legends. Stories of two women, separated by time and circumstance, but brought together by coincidence to haunt a stretch of road called Cline Avenue.

Cline Avenue is one of the main roadways stretching from Gary almost to the Illinois border. Today, a drive down the road provides an unbroken view of urban development and decay. Junk yards and smokestacks seem to stretch as far as the eye can see on either side of the road. However, if the old tales of the road are to be believed, there is something else in the area as well: a ghostly duo that have become the most famous of all the Calumet region's haunts.

'La Llorona' Visits Cudahee

The first phantom matron is a dark, forbidding apparition said to haunt the stretch of Cline Avenue that winds its way through the old Gary neighborhood of Cudahee near Fifth Avenue. Today, most of it is gone, but in the 1940s Cudahee was a thriving neighborhood predominantly made up of Mexican immigrants who came north to work in the steel mills. Some believe that when they transplanted their families and culture into the Calumet region, they brought with them the legend of "La Llorona" or the 'Crying One.'

The tale of La Llorona is an ancient legend of Mexico. It is a story of tragedy, madness, and unspeakable cruelty. The story tells of a young widow who lived with her two young sons in a small town on the outskirts of Mexico City.

One day while in the market place, she caught the eye of a young nobleman from one of the most powerful families in all of Mexico. The man arranged to meet the young mother and the woman soon found herself being lavishly entertained at his palatial home. Before long they were lovers. Soon the young mother was dreaming of the day when they would marry and she and her children could escape the desperate poverty in which they lived.

That day, however, would never come. One night, after dinner in his luxurious mansion, the poor widow confessed her dreams to her handsome young admirer and asked when they would marry. To her shock, the young man sneered at the idea. He could never marry her, he said. When pressed for a reason, the young man said that his family would never approve of the marriage because of her children. They would never accept children fathered by a common peasant into their home. Besides, he explained, her children might one day challenge the inheritance of any children they might have together.

The young widow was distraught when she left the mansion that night. Seeing all of her hopes and dreams dashed, she ran toward her village, her despondency and shock turning to madness. In her demented mind, she saw her children as the stumbling block that kept her from the man she loved and the life of which she dreamed. She determined that the stumbling block must be removed. Quietly slipping into her small adobe hut so as not to awaken her sleeping sons, she quickly found a small knife. Then, stealing silently to their bedsides, she murdered each of her sons in turn.

Her white dress stained crimson with the blood of her innocent sons, she ran back to the home of her lover. Bursting in, she swept past the startled servants and ran to his bedroom. Eyes gleaming with madness, she told him of her deed, and demanded that now, surely, they should be married. The nobleman was horrified. Calling his servants, he had her thrown from the house and then quickly rode to awaken the local priest to confess his inadvertent part in the murder.

Now totally bereft of her senses, the despondent widow wandered the streets, her hands and dress still bearing the stain of her crime. For the next several days, she was seen rambling through the streets of Mexico City, wearing the bloodstained white dress, crying for her children. Eventually, the story of her misdeed reached the local authorities and an order was given to find and arrest her. Before she could be captured, however, the body of the unfortunate widow was found floating in an irrigation ditch near her home.

According to the legend, it is her spirit that still haunts the streets of Mexico City. Stories have been passed down of a woman in white who is seen late at night in the old section of the city, crying piteously for her children, her dress and hands stained with the blood of her young sons. For centuries she has been called "La Llorona," the crying one.

Perhaps, as some suggest, it is this story that formed the basis for the tales of a mysterious woman dressed in white who is said to periodically appear by the side of Cline Avenue as it passes through the old Mexican neighborhood of Cudahey. Over the years, the Mexican inhabitants of the area have given this ghost the name of the woman of ancient lore, "La Llorona," and perhaps this American legend is nothing more than a reflection of the more ancient Mexican tradition.

However, one would be hard pressed to explain that to those who claim to have encountered the spirit. According to local legend, motorists on Cline Avenue have frequently seen her, standing by the side of the road late at night, only to have her disappear into the darkness when she was approached.

Police are said to have been called more than once to the neighborhood to help search for the this mysterious woman after she has appeared to a passing motorist.

Some describe her as being short and thin with a dark complexion and piercing eyes that seem to gleam with madness. Frequently, the stories say there are dark stains on her dress and hands. Others tell of her making wild motions toward those who stop to assist her and screaming something about her children before disappearing into the night. No one, however, has ever reported speaking to her, nor has anyone been able to give an earthly explanation for her sudden disappearances.

Not all agree with the proposed connection between the Mexican legend of La Llorona and the Cudahee phantom. Some Anglo residents of the area claim that the ghost existed long before the first Mexican immigrants moved to the area. Instead, they tell the story of a young mother, driving between Gary and Hammond with her three young children, who missed a turn and swerved off the road. The mother was thrown clear of the wreck but her children were all killed. After the burial of the children, their mother, unhinged by the experience, returned to the spot again and again in a vain search for her lost family. Local residents would often see her wandering the area, totally bereft of her sanity. It was said that she continued her search long after her death in the early 1930s.

Who is the grim specter that haunts this section of Cline Avenue? Is she a figure from an old Mexican story, transplanted by immigrants, or the spirit of an older inhabitant? The debate has raged for years. In reality, no one will ever know. Perhaps, it does not even matter.

However, for many years, dozens and sometimes hundreds of cars have parked along this dark stretch of Cline Avenue on Halloween, in hopes of catching a glimpse of the mysterious woman. In the mid 1960s, a local radio reporter led a group to the area in an effort to investigate the haunting. However, La Llorona, ever mysterious and evasive, was not to be seen. Still, on cool summer evenings, she is said to appear, grim and agitated, by the side of the road outside the neighborhood of Cudahee, her eyes gleaming with a fiery madness. It might seem as though she seeks to tell a story that has been lost in time, to seek revenge for a cruel twist of fate, or perhaps atone for a sin that has bound her forever to a lonely stretch of urban highway.

The Spectral Bride of Cline Avenue

While the identity of the Cudahee ghost will forever remain a mystery, one thing that can be said with certainty is that, if local ghost lore is to be believed, she is not alone. Further west along Cline Avenue, as it nears Hammond, another ghostly woman is said to have taken up residence. Like the mysterious Crying One, her presence is decided otherworldly, and like the woman of Mexican lore, her story speaks of heart-rending tragedy. However, where the narrative of La Llorona has a sinister quality, the second legend echoes to a more sorrowful note. According to legend, she is the ghost of a young Polish woman whose story is one of ill-fated love and a passionate sorrow that goes beyond life and death.

Today, as throughout its history, Hammond is inhabited by a great many families of Polish descent. It was these hard-working adoptive citizens who arrived in the first days of the region's industrial boom to work the factories and build the towns of East Chicago, Whiting, and Hammond. Stoutly religious and clannish by nature, the Polish communities that came to dot northwest Indiana were well-ordered and straightlaced and tended to keep to themselves.

The young lady in question was from one such Polish family in eastern Hammond. Born the only daughter to immigrant parents, she was the jewel of her parents life. Named Sophia after a maternal aunt, she grew into a quiet, obedient, and lovely girl with long blond hair and large blue eyes.

By the age of seventeen she was a beauty and young men from the area began to call on her. Despite the fact that Sophia gently refused the attentions of all those who pursued her, her parents still looked forward to the day when she would pick a husband from the legions of young Polish men who came courting. Then she would marry and begin a family of her own. However, a secret that the young woman bore would dash their dreams and plunge her headlong into tragedy.

Unbeknownst to her family and friends, Sophia had already met and fallen deeply in love with a young man from neighboring Whiting. He was older, nearly twenty-three years of age, and her parents would not have approved of such an age difference. But what forever sealed the fate of this relationship was that she came from proud Polish stock while he was from one of the Puerto Rican families that had recently begun to move to the area. In a time in America when cultural pluralism was virtually unknown, a marriage between these two cultures would have been regarded as scandalous for all concerned.

From the onset, both understood that their parents would neither accept nor support such a relationship and so they vowed to keep their love a secret. However, like Romeo and Juliet of Shakespearean fame, the sparks of their illicit love were only fanned into even more passionate flame by the secrecy in which they were forced to cloak it.

For months they met in secret, stealing away at every opportunity for clandestine trysts. Since neither wished to be seen by friends in their communities, they would often meet by the banks of the Calumet River just south of Cline Avenue as it approached the outskirts of Hammond. Today this area is an industrial wasteland, but in that day the river still retained some of its natural beauty and foliage. By the banks of the Calumet they walked and talked and dreamed of a day when they could be together. As the summer moon reflected off the river, they pledged their love to each other and swore that a way would be found to marry.

Gradually, a plan was developed. It pained Sophia to deceive her parents in such an important matter, but she knew that if her family learned of her relationship with her lover, they would take steps to ensure that she never saw him again. Desperately, she rationalized that if a way could be found for them to marry, perhaps in time her family would come to accept the match.

A priest in nearby Griffith was contacted and told of the couple's intention to marry. At first adverse to marrying them without the consent of their parents, the priest relented when they told him in no uncertain terms that the couple would be wed, if not in a church then by a justice of the peace. Deciding that a church wedding, even under less than ideal circumstances, was better than a secular ceremony, the priest agreed to marry the couple. It was a reckless plan, sure to bring the wrath of both families. What no one could guess at the time, however, is that it would lead to tragedy, death and ultimately, even perhaps to supernatural consequences.

Sophia worked part-time for a local grocer and she had been secreting away a portion of her pay for a simple wedding dress she had seen in a local store window. As the day approached, the prospective bride resisted the temptation to share her secret even with her closest friends, instead wrapping herself in her dreams of a new future with her husband.

Finally, in late September the long-awaited day arrived. Weeks before, Sophia had informed her parents that she would be working at the grocery store a little later than usual on that day and would then travel to a friend's home to spend the night.

When she left the house that day she carried with her a small bag with some of her most precious belongings and the money she had been saving for her dress. Stopping first at the dressmaker's store, she purchased the dress that she had been dreaming of for so long. She then hailed a cab, which took her to the church. There Sophia dressed herself in her beautiful new bridal gown, carefully arranged her hair, and went into the sanctuary to await the coming of her groom. Some say she waits still.

No one knows what happened to the prospective groom on that fated day. Some of the stories say that, rushing toward the church, he was involved in an accident that killed him instantly. Others suggest that it was an industrial accident in the mill where he was working that took his life the day before he was to marry. Still others say that he simply got cold feet and moved from the area, never to return.

Cline Avenue Bridge
Photograph by Kris Harrison

Whatever the case, when the young man had not arrived a full two hours after his appointed time, the kindly priest was forced to advise the young woman that she was waiting in vain. Seeing Sophia weeping and shaken, the priest offered to take her to his office, where they could have tea and talk things over.

Angrily Sophia refused. There had been some mistake, she said. Her lover would never have abandoned her. Gently the priest offered to take her back to her home in Hammond, but again he was rebuffed. Still wearing what would have been her wedding dress, Sophia ran from the church that night and hailed a passing cab. Throwing herself in the back, she asked the driver to take her to Hammond. Already she was picturing her parents anger when they discovered her aborted plan. When word of her humiliation leaked out into her tight-knit community, she would be ostracized. Suddenly, Sophia knew she could never return home.

As the cab turned west onto Cline Avenue and began to pass close by the Calumet River where she and her lover had spent so many precious moments, Sophia made a rash decision. She ordered the cab to the side of the road, opened the door and swept out, heading toward the river. The driver, perplexed, yelled for her to stop, but Sophia ran onward into the darkness. Within a few moments she was on the banks of the river at the exact spot where she and her young man had sworn their love to each other just a few short weeks before.

With a cry of desperation that echoed along the banks Sophia waded into the cold water. When the water was up to her knees, she paused, peered at the full moon for one last bitter moment, and then plunged on. Twenty feet from shore she lost her footing and fell forward into the swirling water. Her instinct for survival flared and she struggled for breathe, but the weight of her dress hindered her and the current drew her deeper into the water. In a few moments her mouth filled with water and her struggles ceased. The full moon, coming out from behind a cloud, shone down on a limp figure in white drifting listlessly downstream.

When Sophia did not come home the next morning, her family began a search. It was not until mid-morning that her mother, searching Sophia's room, came across her diary and learned the truth of her daughters dreams and plans. The police were contacted and eventually the cab driver came forward with his story. Two days later, the girl's body was identified at the Lake County morgue. It had been found by fishermen floating face down along the shore of the Calumet River.

The girl was buried in a Hammond cemetery with the full rites of the Roman Catholic Church. As her casket was lowered into the damp earth, prayers were intoned for the eternal rest of the ill-fated young woman. However, if the stories whispered in the region of her Hammond home are true, rest still seems to be denied her.

It is her spirit, they claim, that is often seen on Cline Avenue as it passes close to the Calumet River. Passing motorists have seen a beautiful girl wearing a wedding dress standing by the side of the road, staring pitifully at the passing motorists before she plunges down the embankment toward the river.

One cab driver had an even closer encounter with the woman in the white dress. Late one night in November, the cab driver was driving along Cline Avenue toward Hammond to pick up a fare. As he drove through the chill evening, a thin drizzle formed out of the dark skies and a mist swept out of the river and clung to the roadside. Slowing for a potentially treacherous curve, the driver was bewildered to see the form of a young girl appear out of the mist by the side of the road. Instinctively he slowed and flicked on his bright lights in an effort to see her more clearly.

By the light of his headlamps, she appeared young with long hair. Most startlingly, she wore a long white dress in the manner of wedding dresses from decades before. For an instant, she was illuminated in the light and then she was gone. The driver slowed further but then, deciding that his mind was playing tricks on him, he pressed the accelerator and moved on toward Hammond.

The cabbie might have written the vision off as a trick of the light and mist except for something that happened a half mile or so from where he had seen the girl. As he drove on through the night, concentrating on the road before him and his waiting customer, he gradually became aware of a damp, cold feeling permeating through the car. At first he thought the window was cracked, admitting the night air, but upon checking, he found this was not the case. The window on the passenger's side of the car was also tightly closed. Thinking perhaps that the rear passenger's door was ajar, the driver stole a glance over his shoulder into the back seat. As he did so, his heart nearly stopped.

He was staring directly into the eyes of a young girl. She sat, staring silently ahead into the night, her eyes glazed and apparently oblivious to her surroundings. Though the night was dark and the interior light of the car was shut off, he could see her clearly. In an instant, he knew that this was the face of the girl he had seen a moment before, standing by the side of the road. As he later told friends, she was totally wet, her once beautiful white dress soiled and dank. Suddenly the smell of river water filled the car.

As might be imagined, the driver was shocked beyond belief. Swerving sharply to the right across two lanes of traffic, he nearly drove off the road in an effort to stop his vehicle. When his car had stopped, he finally dared to take a look into the back of the car once more, but she was gone. No trace of her remained, except for the vague smell of soiled clothing and river water.

While this has been the most dramatic encounter with the ghost of the poor young woman, it has not been the only such sighting. In the early seventies, just before Halloween, a young man and several friends were driving west along Cline Avenue near the river. They were headed toward Hammond to pick up a friend for an evening's revelry. Across the roadway that night lay a fog—common enough near the river in autumn.

However, as they approached Hammond, the driver was terrified to see the form of a young woman, dressed in an old-fashioned white gown, fashion itself out of the fog and float across the road directly into his path. Unable to avoid the form, the young man applied his brakes and the car began to slip sideways. As the car careened forward it seemed to pass directly through the figure, leaving no sound, damage, or body in its wake.

Badly frightened, the young man and his friends drove on to Hammond. There, the boys recounted their experience to their friend and his parents. To their credit, the parents did not seem to doubt the tale told by the boys. Instead the couple, from an old Polish family in the area, simply assured the young men that they had encountered the infamous phantom of Cline Avenue.

Throughout the years, the stories have continued to filter down through the community and others have reported seeing the mysterious lady on Cline Avenue just where it nears the Calumet River. Indeed, she has become a fixture of the local culture and folklore. With the passage of time the story has become modified and the identity of the ghost sometimes confused. However, in the old Polish neighborhoods of Hammond and East Chicago, the "truth" is known. The truth of a sad, sorrowful girl and an ill-fated love that propelled her from her home and life and into the pages of Indiana ghost lore forever.

> *Northwest Indiana is an area unto itself. A sprawling, industrialized complex, there seems little room for whim or fancy. The wind carries with it a reminder of the nature of the region and the glowing lights on the horizon are not the romantic Northern Lights but instead the reflection from the blast furnaces in the distance.*
>
> *Yet even in this urban setting ghost lore abounds — especially on one well-traveled road called Cline Avenue where the legends persist of two women whose lives, and deaths, are bound together in tragedy. Two female specters tied to the area by their fate and eternally bound together as the 'Cline Avenue Ghosts.'*[11]

PART V
HAUNTED LANDMARKS

The Ghost in the Hayloft

Whistling Past the Graveyard

The Wolf Man of Versailles

The Gray Lady of Willard Library

Indiana is a land filled with tradition and history. Far from the generic midwestern state that many assume it to be, the state of Indiana is filled with unique places, each with its own special significance and lore attached to it. From great monuments to battlefields to the famous covered bridges of Brown County, the landscape of Indiana is a rich mosaic of fascinating and colorful landmarks. If these landmarks could but speak, they would tell tales of great deeds and sweeping history. More than a few of them, however, might tell tales of a more uncanny nature as well. Strange stories that stretch the imagination and tell of dark, forbidding events.

Included here are just a few of these landmarks. From a private library to a restaurant to an eerie cemetery to the natural beauty of some of our state parks, each story contains within it but a flavor of our history and traditions. Something of our history and culture that reaches out from the past to cling to our time like a shroud.

The Ghost in the Hayloft

Indiana can boast of a great many specialty restaurants which have sprung up in old jails, abandoned factories and, in at least one case — the Hayloft Restaurant in Plymouth — a restored nineteenth century barn. Built in the late 1800s, the huge stone and wood structure was a functioning barn until the early 1970s when it was painstakingly restored as a restaurant. Thoroughly comfortable, yet elegant in style, the Hayloft has managed to keep much of it's rustic ambiance and charm. However, if the tales told about the Hayloft are true, as many believe, then it has also retained something else from its past — a restless spirit that is a remnant of a bygone day and age — a presence that reaches out to touch the lives of the living in subtle — and not-so-subtle ways.

Rachel McCormick* is the current owner of the Hayloft. When she purchased the eatery in 1989 from the Cook family who had first acquired and renovated it, she was unaware of the ghostly reputation of the place. "I first heard of the haunting," she now recalls, "from several of the staff who had stayed over from when the Cooks owned the restaurant. They told me that there was a ghost in the building, and that they had named him 'Homer'. It was just a name they came up with sort of as a joke."

The staff also informed Rachel that, according to legend, the ghost was that of a former owner of the farm who had died of a heart attack in the barn. Rachel was inclined at first to ignore the old stories, concerning herself instead with the business of taking over the busy restaurant. But before long, she and her staff began to experience occurrences that brought the tales back to mind.

Most of the inexplicable events seem to occur in an upstairs dining room called the 'Silo Room.' The first disturbance that Rachel became aware of was reported to her by two employees who were working in this room prior to opening one night. "At the time the employees came to me and told me that they had been setting up the room for the night. The restaurant was not open yet and all the doors were locked. Suddenly, both of them saw a man in bib overalls walk into the room from the stairway entrance. They were startled because they knew the place was locked up and besides, they should have heard someone walking up the stairs. He walked to the middle of the room and suddenly disappeared. It was like he just suddenly wasn't there."

Exterior of the Haylot Resaturant
Courtesy of Hayloft Restaurant

This was not to be the ghost's last appearance in the Silo Room. Not long afterward, a busboy was leaving the building late one night after finishing his duties. "There is a door from that room out to the parking lot," Rachel explains. "The staff often leave that way when they are done for the night and tell the dishwasher to lock up after they are gone."

That night, as the busboy made his way through the dimly-lit room toward the outside door he was surprised to see the figure of a man in overalls standing between him and the exit. Realizing that there should be no such person in the restaurant after hours, the startled young man took a step backward only to have the figure disappear into thin air. The busboy beat a hasty retreat down the front stairs to another exit and quit his job shortly thereafter.

Other staff have related to Rachel that they too have seen the ghost and all describe him as an older man dressed in bib overalls, much as a farmer might dress. One similar and somewhat unsettling element in all the stories is that, true to classical ghostly tradition, the witnesses report that although the figure is clearly visible—except for the feet. The figure ends just below the knees.

Other ghostly manifestations have occurred in the restaurant as well. Frequently the ghost has been known to move objects in the restaurant in a playful manner. "The first experience I ever personally witnessed here," Rachel recalls, "was one night shortly after buying the place when I was closing up. It was late and I knew that I was alone. I went into the kitchen to make sure all the burners were turned off on the stove. I was bent over checking the burners when I heard a stack of heavy pewter plates next to the stove start rattling. I got up in a hurry and as I did, they stopped. Just as a joke, I called out, 'Homer, don't do that again.' When nothing happened for a minute, I sort of flippantly said 'chicken ghost!' As soon as I said that, I saw the plates start to jump and rattle. These were heavy plates and there is no way that a simple vibration from outside could move them like that. I stood there and watched them jump around for a moment and then they quit and I got the heck out of there."

Rachel has not been the only one to see things move of their own volition in the restaurant. One guest came to Steve McCormick*, Rachel's husband, and told him that during his last visit to the restaurant, he had seen a vase of silk flowers float from one side of the dining room to another, a distance of over twenty feet. Surprisingly, the man did not seem upset by the incident. Instead, he later returned and asked to be seated in the same booth in case Homer would make a return appearance. The man left disappointed.

Routinely, the staff has also reported objects moved or suddenly 'misplaced' from their customary location, only to reappear elsewhere. Kitchen utensils are sometimes found missing from a spot where they had just been placed, only to reappear in an unlikely location. Kitchen staff report that pots and pans occasionally have been known to fall from racks when no one was in their vicinity.

Interior of Hayloft Restaurant
Courtesy of Hayloft Resaturant

One kitchen worker comments: "If this had happened once or twice, you might write it off as a coincidence, but it happens far too often. Once, when the restaurant was being set up for the evening, I went into the bar area and was talking with one of the busboys. He asked me if Homer was around, and I said

'I haven't seen him but I'm sure he's here somewhere.' Just then I heard a clanging noise and when I went back into the kitchen, three of the pots had fallen from their racks. I personally had put them there the night before and I'm sure they were secure. The kitchen was empty, and I know that no one had been in there."

Indeed, the resident ghost of the Hayloft seems to sometimes respond when his name is mentioned. Rachel reports: "A lot of times, if his name is mentioned, glassware will break almost immediately for no apparent reason. I don't know if he likes to be talked about or not."

Another employee who formerly worked in the restaurant relates a somewhat humorous account of the ghost's propensity to move objects. While working in the bar area one night, he spoke with a patron about the ghost. "This middle aged man was sitting at the bar smoking cigarettes and putting the ashes in an ashtray next to him on the bar. We were always careful to put an ashtray next to someone who was smoking because we did not want the bar marred up with burn marks," he recalls. "I had just served him a drink and he commented that he had recently heard that the place was supposed to be haunted. I told him that I had not seen or heard anything unusual in the restaurant. 'Yeah, I'm sure you won't,' replied the patron. 'Personally, I think this ghost business is just bull anyway.' Just then, he went to put out his cigarette without looking down and ground it out on the bar top. The ash tray had slid down the bar a good three feet without either of us seeing it. The man looked at the ash tray, looked at me, and said, 'I've got to go!' I was not a bit worried about his driving. I think he sobered up real quick that night."

So frequent have the occurrences been that they have become more or less routine to the staff. Staff members have been known to speak to the ghost on occasion when something mysterious occurs. As one dishwasher put it, "It's no big deal. Something will happen and I'll say 'Homer, I have work to do. Cut it out now.' And generally, he will."

Overall, the ghost seems to confine his activities to the kitchen and second floor dining room. However, on occasion he has been seen and heard in different locations throughout the building. "He has been seen twice in the parking lot," Mrs. McCormick relates, "and several times in an upstairs hallway." However often the spirit has been seen, Rachel says that he is more frequently heard. "The footsteps are the most common thing," she says. "Often I have been upstairs in my office during the day when I knew no one is around and I will hear this heavy tread of footsteps coming up the stairs. It is very clear — I can almost tell you which stair he is on. But no one ever appears and I am alone in the building."

Delores Boggs, who has worked in the restaurant since 1992, also reports hearing the footsteps. "I have heard them frequently," Mrs. Boggs says. "They are of a large man — I would guess about a 200 to 250 pounds. It sounds like someone wearing a big shoe or more likely a boot."

As a cook at the restaurant, Mrs. Boggs is frequently asked to close up the restaurant after everyone has left for the night. She relates that sometimes after carefully checking the restaurant she will exit only to immediately hear footsteps echoing through the empty rooms she has just left. "I know there is no one in the building, so I just leave the place to him," she says with an air of resignation.

Mrs. Boggs seems to have had a great many experiences with the ghost but says that when she began work in the restaurant she knew nothing of the legends attached to the place. "I had no idea there was a ghost around," she says. This changed, however, late one winter night when she was closing up after hours. "I had locked up and gone out into the parking lot. It was a cold night and snow had been falling all evening. The parking lot was empty except for my car and I knew that there was no one around."

She was understandably shocked then when, as she walked toward her car, she became aware of a man standing at the edge of the parking lot intently watching her. "He was a big man in overalls," she recalls, "and he was just standing there staring at me. I was a woman alone and I was frightened. I ran to my car and unlocked the door, all the time keeping my eyes on the man. When I got to my car, suddenly he just disappeared — vanished." Thoroughly frightened, Mrs. Boggs sat in her car trying to calm her badly shaken nerves. She knew what she had seen, yet the man's sudden disappearance seemed odd, to say the least.

"Finally, my curiosity got the best of me," she says. "I got out of the car and went to the place I had seen the man. There was an inch of fresh snow on the ground yet there were no footprints at all in the snow. It was like he had never been there." Since that snowy night, Mrs. Boggs reports frequent sightings of the ghost. "I will see him out of the corner of my eye," she says, "and I will turn and he is gone." She has also seen him walk, on at least one occasion, from the kitchen area into the bar only to dissolve into thin air.

Mrs. Boggs has also been present when objects moved apparently on their own power. Once while upstairs in the bar area talking with a co-worker, Mrs. Boggs and her friend were startled to see a carton of dish soap she had just placed on the bar inch over to the edge of the bar and fall to the floor. In addition, Mrs. Boggs and other kitchen staff, have been present when pots and pans have mysteriously taken flight from their racks.

Another strange sensory experience is also related by Mrs. Boggs. "I can smell a peculiar odor when he is around," she reflects. "Others have smelled it too. It is not a bad odor, just an earthy kind of smell. Someone told me that they thought it smelled like wood burning, but that is not quite it. It is a very unique smell. I'll notice it and I know that he is around." Frequently the smell occurs when no one is in the area and no normal explanation can be found.

Mrs. Boggs has become accustomed to, even comfortable with, the phantom and apparently he feels much the same way toward her. This can be seen in a minor but interesting event that occurred not long ago in the restaurant. "I was busy in the kitchen," says Mrs. Boggs. "I was carrying a load of dishes to a cart and when I went to put them down, I found that someone had left an empty box in the cart where the dishes were to go. It was a bother because I would have to put the stack of dishes down and move the box. Anyway, I turned to put the dishes down and when I turned back, the box had moved itself out of the way. I felt the ghost was being helpful, so I said 'thanks!' and went back to work."

It is through Mrs. Bogg's affinity with the spirit that a bit more may have been learned with regard to his identity. "I am part Cherokee Indian," Mrs. Boggs explains. "I don't know if that has anything to do with it, but I seem to have a sense of these sorts of things. I talk to him, and even though I do not hear him exactly, I think that he is answering."

Perhaps this explains why Mrs. Boggs came to with an idea of who was haunting the restaurant. "Delores came to me," Rachel remembers, "and told me that she had this strong feeling that the ghost was not named Homer. That did not surprise me because Homer was just a name that had been given him. She told me that she thought his name was Jacob*, that he had lived and died around the barn and that he was a deeply religious man."

These feelings, Mrs. Boggs relates, simply came to her as she worked around the restaurant. "I did not think much of it at the time," Rachel continues, "but several months later, two ladies came into the restaurant. I spoke with them and they told me that they were relatives of the family that had originally owned the barn and the attached farm. I asked them about the man who had owned the farm and they told me that he was a large man who had died of natural causes while in the barn. I asked them what his name was and they said 'Jacob.' I then asked them if he had been a religious person in life. 'Oh yes, you have no idea!' was their reply."

As sometimes happens with people who work around paranormal occurrences, the staff of the Hayloft take their resident spirit as part and parcel of the restaurant itself. "No one around here is particularly frightened by him," says one worker. "He is just a part of the place."

Delores Boggs puts it another way. "I get the feeling that he is just a hard-working man who wants to finish whatever it is he started here," she says. "He's not angry or vindictive—he simply has unfinished business in this place." What unfinished business this might be remains a mystery but perhaps this is as close to an explanation for the strange events surrounding the Hayloft as ever will be forthcoming.

Indiana can boast of a great number of fine restaurants, each with its own ambiance and unique character. Amid the farmlands and fields just outside of Plymouth, there lies a singular restaurant with an aura all its own. Rough-hewn yet elegant, rustic yet comfortable, the Hayloft creates a unique atmosphere. Further, according the legends, new and old, that surround the place, part of that atmosphere may well be a spirit of a farmer who maintains an interest in his former abode. A simple man of the land who has never left the place he loved and thus entered the pages of Indiana ghost lore.[12]

Whistling Past the Graveyard

When traveling past the graveyard late last night
Billy and I had a terrible fright
For there were the dead parading proud
With brackish bone and moldy shroud.
  -Old English Folk Song.

Graveyards are as much a part of traditional ghost lore as rattling chains and decaying mansions. Nearly every small town harbors, somewhere in its vicinity, an ancient cemetery where the weeds grow deep along the wrought iron fence and tall trees cast strange shadows in the moonlight. Stories are whispered about such spots and late night travelers passing these places of the dead may be excused for quickening their pace and keeping their eyes on the path before them.

Throughout the length and breadth of the Hoosier state, stories of haunted graveyards and cemeteries abound. From small family plots to sprawling metropolitan cemeteries, the legends tell that such locations may well harbor dark things better left buried. On the following pages, the reader will meet but a sampling of Indiana's graveyard denizens. Some are stories of justice undone and angry spirits that stalk the night. Some are stories of more genial spirits, content merely to peek around the tombstones or prowl in the vicinity of their earthly remains. All are the stuff of folklore and legend. However, if one were to find himself passing an old country cemetery late at night when the tall grass seems to whisper and the wind moans softly through the trees, it might be well to pause and wonder: "What really lies within these places of the dead?"

Gypsies Graveyard, Crown Point

At first glance, the cemetery outside of Crown Point is like many other country cemeteries. The tall iron fence that surrounds part of the grounds is rusted and tilted. The ancient markers are in disrepair, many broken by age and vandalism. Beneath a full October moon, however, the white tombstones seem to glow with a sullen light and the trees surrounding the fence reach for the sky like barren skeletons. It is in this setting then that residents tell the legend of the 'Gypsies' Graveyard.' It is a story of tragedy born of human intolerance and hatred that ends with a macabre reminder that hatred can bring consequences beyond human understanding.

Crown Point, Indiana is a charming example of a small midwestern town. Located midway between the large metropolitan centers of the Calumet region and the farmlands that lie to the south, Crown Point has managed to maintain a small town ambiance despite its growth in recent years.

With a large old-fashioned courthouse in the town square, Crown Point has an all-American feel. The town's only brush with notoriety came in 1934 when the famed gangster John Dillinger made a daring escape from the local jail with what was later reported to be a gun carved from a bar of soap. In his wake, he managed to leave most of the jail guards locked into the cell he had just vacated. Despite this ignominious fame, however, Crown Point has remained a simple, wholesome community reminiscent of midwestern towns from decades ago. If one travels south and east from the downtown area along a rural stretch of roadway known to locals as 'Nine Mile Stretch,' an age-worn cemetery comes into view.

The story of the cemetery reportedly begins in the early 1800s when Indiana was a busy crossroads for settlers and wagon trains passing through the area heading west. At the time, Crown Point was a small but well-established farming settlement. In the fall of 1820, a very different group of travelers arrived in Crown Point. Dark-skinned and strange of dress, the word quickly spread that a band of gypsies had made their camp southeast of the community.

Long despised and persecuted in their native Europe the Romany, or gypsies, began arriving in America in the early nineteenth century. Unfortunately, despite the 'melting pot' reputation of the United States, gypsies in America often found themselves singled out for the same sort of rebuff they had suffered in their native lands.

In the early 1800s, gypsy bands in caravans of brightly-colored wagons began to traverse the country. Typically such a band consisted of five or six wagons and about thirty men, women and children. They would camp in an unoccupied spot and stay for several weeks before moving on. The gypsies made their meager living selling handmade jewelry, telling fortunes, and selling herbal medicines. Though essentially benign and reserved by nature, the appearance of gypsies was sometimes met with aversion and outright enmity by the local population who considered the gypsies to be thieves, witches — and worse.

It is said this was apparently the case when a band of gypsies appeared near Crown Point. Wary and fearful, the residents of the area kept a safe distance from the strange newcomers. Fantastic tales quickly spread from farmhouse to farmhouse about pagan rituals conducted around gypsy campfires, and of cattle and domestic animals that had reportedly begun to disappear from farms in the area. Police investigated the camp more than once and found no purloined livestock but the collective mind of the community was made up. When a group of the gypsies appeared on the town square and attempted to sell jewelry and herbs they were quickly run off by the local sheriff. Several gypsy women, attending a local market to purchase food and supplies were forced to return empty-handed to their camp.

Perhaps the entire unpleasant episode might have passed with the gypsies pulling up stakes and moving on had not nature and illness taken a hand. Winter came early that year and in early November the weather turned cold. Then, just as today the advent of winter also brought with it sickness—a particularly virulent strain of influenza. While the flu still kills a great many Americans each year, particularly the elderly and infirm, it was even more dangerous in the early years of the nineteenth century. Due to the lack of proper medical knowledge and care, influenza epidemics frequently swept through midwestern settlements taking the lives of thousands.

Gypsies Graveyard. Photograph by Chris Shultz.

This form is being provided as a tool to help you get the most from your visit today. After checking in, but before seeing the doctor, please use your time to answer the questions below.

Dr. _Bill Burns_   Appointment Time: _3:00_   Time Allocated: _____

Write down the reason you came in today.

    Thrush

Are there any other problems you wish to discuss?

    ↓ WBC

What is the most important thing you would like done today?

What prescriptions do you need refilled before your next appointment?

Have you had any lab tests done recently ordered by us or another physician? If yes, for what and where?

Checklist:

- ❏ Do I need a follow up appointment?
- ❏ Do I have orders for tests?
- ❏ Do I need a referral?
- ❏ Do I understand instructions as given?
- ❏ Did I receive prescription refills?
- ❏ Do you need a work or school note written?

The particular tragedy of the 1820 influenza outbreak in Crown Point was that it was a member of the gypsy band who first came down with the illness. Soon many in the gypsy band fell deathly ill. The situation was made much worse because food was scarce and medicine nonexistent in the camp.

The old legend states that when word leaked out of the influenza outbreak an informal quarantine was placed upon the gypsy camp. No one from the neighboring farms was allowed to approach the camp and the town's only physician refused to come and treat the sick. What had previously been ostracism on the part of the community now turned to open hostility.

Finally one night, according to the tale, a group of men from the neighborhood rode silently into the gypsy camp. Dismounting a safe distance from the wagons, the men shouted that they wished to speak with the leader of the gypsy band. An aged man of dark complexion and wearing bright clothing appeared by the fire and announced he would speak for his people.

In no uncertain terms the men spoke their mind. The gypsies were told to leave immediately. They were no longer welcome — if they ever had been welcome. With guns at their sides, the men warned ominously of 'trouble' if the gypsies chose to stay.

Humbly the gypsy leader protested that many in his group were too sick to travel, particularly the women and children who were weak from the influenza and lack of food. Perhaps, he suggested, if food and medicine would be provided to the camp in a week or so they could move on. This suggestion was met with derision. The gypsies were given two days to be gone. No food would be provided them. If they wanted medicine, they could use the herbal remedies they had been trying to sell. With this, the men mounted their horses and were gone.

No one ventured near the camp for two days. Finally, a nearby farmer reported that he had seen the gypsy caravan traveling past his farmhouse late at night. When word of this exodus spread, several men from the community rode out to the camp. They found it deserted with only one trace left of the gypsies presence. As they walked through the tall grass of the former campsite, they spotted several small mounds of earth among the trees at the back of the small meadow. They were graves in which the gypsies had left behind their dead.

Satisfied, the men rode back to their homes. However, upon arriving at their farmhouses each of the men found that, not unreasonably, their trousers were damp from the dew from the grass they had walked through to examine the graves. But they were amazed to find that this time their trousers were stained a bright crimson—the color of blood. As one wife put it, the gypsies had placed a curse on the place, to remind the local inhabitants of their inhospitality.

The story is disputed by many who know the history of the area. A search of local historical records shows no official mention of a visit by gypsies to the area in 1820 or any other time. However, the story has been passed down from generation to generation in Crown Point. The legend also states that the site of the gypsy camp is now the locale of the small country cemetery that is known as the 'Gypsies Graveyard.'

In the rural southeast section of Crown Point the stories persist. There have been reports from those passing by late at night, of a strange camp fire seen in the middle of the graveyard—a campfire that suddenly disappears, evaporating into the mist, leaving no trace behind.

In the late 1970s on a night close to Halloween, a number of teenagers visited the cemetery in an effort to scare the girls among the group. Later they swore they were chased from the grounds by a round ball of glowing light that emerged from the tombstones and flew toward them. One said that the mysterious ball of light chased the car down the road during their hasty departure.

More recently, local resident Larry Wirtz went to the eerie burial ground one evening with a friend. A lifelong resident of Crown Point, Mr. Wirtz entertained his friend by telling him the old legend of the Gypsies' Graveyard as they walked among the tombstones. "It was sort of uneventful," Mr. Wirtz now remembers. "But when we got back into the car, my friend looked down at his pants and his eyes got big. The bottom of his legs were stained red — just like blood. What is even stranger is that mine were not. But then again, I have some gypsy blood in me. I guess they took it easy on me!"

> *The story of the Gypsies' Graveyard lives on, but the historical authenticity of this tale is in question. What is known is that human intolerance, bigotry, and suspicion of those different than ourselves has not been erased in the 120 years since the story began. And who knows but that such evil, born in the hearts of men, might have ramifications in places like the Gypsies' Graveyard.*[13]

The Ghostly Mother of Stepp Cemetery

Driving through Morgan Monroe State Forest near Bloomington, one is apt of find oneself traveling past a small cemetery lying serenely in the midst of the deep forest. A few white tombstones huddle together near the center of the cemetery. On the brightest summer days the cemetery is illuminated with sunshine for only a few hours of the day. The rest of the time, the deep shadows from the trees blanket the grounds in leafy shadow. It is a peaceful and beautiful spot to while away eternity.

On the edge of that cemetery, next to a small grave, there sits a strange object that has been the subject of much speculation over the years. It is the stump of a fallen tree which has been crafted with great care into the form of a chair. Over the years, it has become known as the 'Witch's Throne.' However, if the ghostly tale that is told of this strange perch is true, it is not the seat of a witch at all but of a mother whose tragic love took her beyond the bounds of sanity and into the realm of Indiana ghost lore.

The cemetery in question is known as Stepp Cemetery, after one of the families who first settled the area and whose graves dot the cemetery grounds. Throughout the years, the cemetery has become a sort of landmark in the area. Local legend holds that during the last days of the nineteenth century the site was frequented by a group of 'Jacobites,' a strange quasi-religious group. Local residents recall stories of sheriff's deputies being called to the area to break up orgiastic rites held in the cemetery. However, these stories — as macabre and titillating as they might be — do not serve as the basis for the well-known ghost story that has been told about this graveyard for many years. Instead, the ghost of Stepp Cemetery is part of a tale that is wrapped in sadness, tragedy, and madness.

She was a mother — a woman whose whole life was devoted to her only child, a daughter. Some stories relate that she was from a prominent family in the Boston area; others that she and her husband came from New Albany, or one of the small Indiana towns to the east. Though the passing years have erased her real name, she is often called Anna. Whatever the case, she and her husband, Jacob, arrived in Bloomington in the early 1930s. Here he found employment in the nearby quarry where work was relatively plentiful, even during the Depression.

They settled into a small homestead not far from Bloomington near the Morgan Monroe State Forest. Their lives were tranquil and happy. While work in the quarries was long, backbreaking and sometimes dangerous, employment was steady and the income provided well for a young couple just starting out in life. In time, their home was further blessed by the birth of a daughter, christened Emily after a maiden aunt.

Now the young bride's life was complete. She was devoted to her husband and child and although they had little of the luxuries of life, the small family was content. However, before long fate was to intervene and their happy life was to be destroyed in a cruel manner. The first blow came one night in late November when Jacob failed to return home from work at his regular time. Darkness was coming on fast as Anna nervously scanned the dirt road leading to their farm. Perhaps, she told herself, Jacob had just stopped to visit with some of his co-workers on the way home. Perhaps he was delayed at the quarry. However, as night came she knew in her heart that something was terribly wrong.

Finally, in the distance she saw the headlights of a car traveling toward the house. With relief Anna swept out of the house expecting to see her husband's Model A Ford coming up the narrow drive. She stopped short when she saw it was a car that she did not recognize. The automobile slowly came to a stop and a portly middle-aged stranger emerged. With eyes cast down toward the earth, he introduced himself as the supervisor at the quarry where Jacob worked. Slowly, haltingly, he explained to Anna that Jacob was dead. He had been working in the quarry late that afternoon when a dynamite blast had gone off prematurely, killing him instantly. Reeling, the young mother listened as the man mouthed the condolences of his company. He then handed her an envelope containing two hundred dollars, the sum total of the wages owed to Jacob and a small additional amount paid to the widows of company employees. Finally, he informed her that her husband's body had been taken to a local mortuary where she could claim it, whereupon the supervisor expressed his deep sorrow and took his leave.

Two days later, Jacob's body was buried in Stepp Cemetery not far from the small farm he had shared with his wife and daughter. Because the couple was not well-known in the community, the funeral party consisted only of the funeral director, a pastor from the nearby Methodist church, and Jacob's wife and daughter. After a short, solemn ceremony, the body of Jacob was lowered into the earth and with it Anna's dreams and hopes for happiness.

After her husband's death Anna devoted herself completely to her daughter. If she had been a doting mother before Jacob's death, Anna became totally immersed in her child after he was gone. She became obsessive concerning Emily's safety and well-being. Even after her daughter was of school age, Anna insisted on walking her to and from school every day. When Emily's friends came to play, Anna was always careful to make sure that they stayed near the cabin and could always be seen hovering about keeping a wary eye on her daughter. At night, she would tuck her daughter into bed and sing her to sleep with an old Irish lullaby she had learned from her grandmother. As darkness swept across the small homestead, the sweet, sorrowful notes of the lullaby could be heard floating out through the night.

Even when Emily had reached sixteen years of age her mother's devotion did not wane. Indeed, as her daughter began to mature into a beautiful young woman, Anna became more obsessed than ever with her daughter—even trying to keep her daughter from participating in any social activities, preferring to keep her safe at home. But Anna knew that the day would come when she could no longer keep her daughter to herself. In time she knew her daughter would take an interest in the outside world and, most particularly, in young men.

That day finally came just before Emily's seventeenth birthday. A young man from Bloomington, who had met Emily through friends at her school, came to call on Emily. Though suspicious of the young man's attentions, Anna had to admit that he seemed courteous and respectful. After visiting with both mother and daughter on several occasions, the young man came to Anna and asked if he might escort Emily to a local dance in Bloomington the next night.

It was a question Anna had long dreaded. Her instincts told her to refuse the request. It would be safest, and perhaps best, to keep her daughter at home by her side. However, as she looked at the face of her daughter, so eager and hopeful, Anna knew that she could not deny Emily a life of her own. Against her own wishes and judgment, Anna gave permission for the two to go to the dance the next night. However, she placed strict guidelines on the date. The young man must have Emily back to her home no later than 10:00 p.m. If she was to come home any later, the young man would find himself unwelcome in Anna's home and no further contact with Emily would be permitted.

The pair readily agreed to the restrictions and the next night, as dusk was beginning to fall across the valley, the young man drove his father's 1940 Packard down the dusty road to the farm. It was autumn and the forest around was full of color and beauty. Still nothing could match the beauty of the young girl waiting expectantly by the door of the farmhouse. She wore a plain calico dress, but even in the gathering darkness the young man could see her dark eyes and a smile that seemed to light up the night. Anna again admonished the couple to be back by 10:00 p.m. at the latest, and with a mixture of pride and apprehension she watched as they drove down the road. She would never see her daughter alive again.

They say that the car crash that killed Emily and her date was caused by the weather. It had been raining since mid-evening and the roads had become slick. However, haste was undoubtedly a contributing factor as well. The couple had stayed longer than they intended at the dance and were speeding back to the farm to comply with the 10:00 p.m. curfew when the car slid off the road. It crashed headlong into a tree and caught fire. Ironically, it was Anna's own dictum, made out of concern for her daughter's safety, that had led to the girl's demise.

Two days later, another funeral was held at Stepp Cemetery. It was reminiscent of the scene that had occurred years earlier when Jacob's body was laid to rest. Now, however, it was the body of young Emily that was buried just a short distance from her father's grave.

Emily's death was the final blow for Anna — she had lost her last shred of happiness in life. As she stood silently watching the coffin containing the remains of her daughter being lowered into the ground she knew that she was burying her own life as well. At that moment, Anna lost her reason for living. Some say she lost her sanity as well.

Anna would never recover from her daughter's death. She became a total recluse, never venturing far from her home. The few who saw her said that she always wore mourning clothes, a long black dress and bonnet. Growing her own vegetables in a small garden behind her house, Anna never was seen in town or at the small Methodist meeting house she and Emily had formerly attended. Indeed, the only place she was ever seen, outside her farm, was Stepp Cemetery.

After the death of her husband, Anna and Emily had frequently visited Jacob's grave to tend to the weeds and to place wildflowers near the small headstone. With the death of Emily, however, Anna began to visit the graves daily. There she would sit for hours on end, reclining on the smooth grass next to her daughter's grave talking to Emily as though she was still alive.

Eventually, Anna found a more comfortable setting for her visits. One spring shortly after Emily's untimely demise, lightning struck and felled a tree not far from her daughter's grave. After the tree was hauled away, a jagged blackened stump remained standing upright that resembled a crude chair. Taking a sharp knife and hatchet with her to the cemetery, Anna carefully carved and shaped the stump into a seat from which she could comfortably view the graves of her daughter and husband.

Those passing by the cemetery began to see the figure of a woman in black sitting on her 'throne' at one end of the cemetery. Sometimes they reported hearing the sounds of an ancient Irish lullaby echoing out from the cemetery grounds. If Anna was approached, she would run away to a nearby grove of trees where she would hide, staring ominously at the visitors until their departure. Locals began to avoid the cemetery and said that the old woman who frequented it was crazy. It was best to leave the woman in black alone.

The date and cause of Anna's death is not known. It is said that she died just a few years after her daughter. It is supposed that she was buried in Stepp Cemetery with her daughter and husband, but no marker can be found for her. No record of her burial was ever made and no obituary was ever recorded. Perhaps this sad, melancholy lady slipped into death as silently and sorrowfully as she had lived her life. Perhaps in death she found some measure of the peace that life had denied her. Or perhaps not.

It is said that the woman in black returns — or more accurately — never left. Since the 1950s, rumors of a strange woman seen in Stepp Cemetery at night have swept through Bloomington. Some call her a witch because she is always seen in a long black dress and bonnet. The charred stump she sits upon has become known as the 'Witch's Throne.'

The story has been handed down through generations of high school students that if you touch the Witch's Throne under a full moon, you will die a violent death within a year. Teenagers have dared each other to drive into the cemetery late at night to see the witch. Most have come back disappointed but through the years a few have come back shaken, having seen a dark figure rise from the seat and move toward them out of the darkness.

Others report a curious phenomenon associated with the mound of earth next to the chair, which is reputed to be the grave of Anna's ill-fated daughter. It is said that if an object is placed on the grave at nightfall it will invariably be found to have been moved from the grave the next morning, even if watch is kept outside the cemetery all night to preclude any human interference. Anna, it seems, is still guarding the remains of her beloved Emily.

Others have reported hearing strange sounds emanating from the cemetery grounds, particularly late at night. Local law enforcement officials are said to have received reports of the sound of a woman's sobbing cries sounding through the night. Others, driving by the site in the early hours of the morning have reported hearing the haunting melody of a lullaby coming to their ears from the darkness of the cemetery grounds.

Through the years, Stepp Cemetery has become quite a landmark in the Bloomington area. Now part of the Morgan Monroe State Forest, the cemetery is a frequent stop for both the curious and those interested in the folklore of the region. The headstones are weathered and gray, most having been rendered illegible by the ravages of time, yet the 'throne,' and the legend surrounding it, remain.

> *In one corner of the cemetery near a gently mounded patch of earth, there remains the curious stump of a long-dead tree that has been fashioned into a kind of seat or throne. Some say that it is the throne of a witch. The older residents of the area, however, tell a very different story. They know that it is the seat of a sorrowful woman who comes to guard over the graves of her loved ones. A solitary, enigmatic spirit still seeking the peace and love she was denied in life, she carries within her a fierce grief that has taken her beyond the bounds of life and death and into Indiana ghost lore.*[14]

The Wolf Man of Versailles

Of all the state parks in Indiana, Versailles State Park is one of the most beautiful. Its 5,905 acres of gently rolling hills and valleys, most covered with deep woods, are a reminder of what the Hoosier state looked like before the advent of settlers and civilization. In one of these valleys, Bat Cave, one of the largest and perhaps the best known caves in the state, is a natural wonder that draws cave enthusiasts, or spelunkers, from across the midwest. Throughout the decades thousands of tourists have flocked to Versailles State Park and to Bat Cave, but few know the legend of Silas Shimmerhorn, a mysterious man who, it is said, still treads the paths of Versailles State Park.

As his truck bumped along the dark road, the Park Ranger looked at the full moon floating in the dark sky. Regretfully, he thought for a moment of all the places he would rather be on a Saturday night than chasing down ridiculous reports from hysterical campers. It was preposterous. A camper had called the ranger station to report hearing the howling of wolves, not one but many, in the vicinity of his camp. The ranger shook his head. It was unlikely that there was even a single wolf in the state park, let alone a pack. The park had its share of deer and raccoons and even some coyotes that still prowled the meadows, but not a wolf pack. The last wolf pack had been driven from southern Indiana decades ago. Surely the camper had heard the howl of coyote, magnified by echoes in the distance. Or perhaps it was just overindulgence in the 'liquid courage' that campers sometimes sneaked into the camp to ward off the chill of night. In either case, it meant that the ranger had to go check out the report.

The ranger maneuvered his truck around a twisting curve and crested a hill. Below him was a large meadow flanked on three sides by dark woods. Suddenly he hit the brakes hard and his truck slid to a stop. The ranger sat silently, gaping at the sight before him. In the light of the full moon, the ranger could see clearly the scene in the meadow below. There *were* wolves. Not just one or two, but an entire pack of twenty or thirty large beasts. From his vantage point he could clearly see that these were not coyotes or stray dogs but large timber wolves on the hunt. The moiling mob of animals ran in all direction in the meadow sniffing the air, as though searching for the scent of game. Suddenly, the night was filled with their cries.

Then the ranger saw something in their midst that took his breath away. Crouched in the midst of the pack was a man. He was naked from the waist up, but his long beard and unkempt hair nearly covered his upper torso. He ran in a half crouch, as though wary of his surroundings, slowly making his way across the meadow.

Suddenly the moon went behind a cloud and the meadow below was cloaked in darkness. Impossibly, when it reappeared a moment later the meadow was empty. Initially the ranger thought perhaps that the wolf pack had run into the woods but he quickly realized that there had not been enough time in the instant of darkness for the entire wolf pack to disappear. On the heels of that realization came another one — one the ranger did not want to accept.

The ranger stared for a moment down onto the empty field then put his truck into drive and began to make his way down the hill. Already however, he knew that he would find no tracks of wolves in the soft earth of the meadow. Already he knew that he would file no report of what he had seen and would say nothing to his supervisor. This was because he knew that Silas Shimmerhorn had returned.

The origins of this legend begin with the bloody Civil War. Ask most Hoosiers what names come to mind when they consider civil war battlefields and most will speak of the great battlefields such as Gettysburg or Shiloh. However, a surprising number of Hoosiers fail to realize that Indiana itself was once directly threatened by the conflict when Morgan's Raiders invaded in 1863.

The war between the states was the most bloody conflict in American history. Waged from 1861 to 1865, the war would cost the lives of over 600,000 young men. Although the Confederate Army was able to win some impressive victories early in the conflict, the tide of war had already begun to turn against the southern cause when the war reached its terrible climax in July of 1863.

Illustration from "The Legend of Bat Cave" in *Outdoor Indiana.*
Courtesy of Indiana Department of Natural Resources.

In the first days of that month the Confederate Army suffered two crucial defeats. On July 3, the Army of Virginia, under General Robert E. Lee, was defeated in the battle of Gettysburg. The next day, July 4, the city of Vicksburg, Mississippi, was taken by Union forces after a siege of forty-seven days. The same day, General John Hunt Morgan of the Confederate Army crossed into Kentucky and began his infamous raid. Morgan had been ordered into Kentucky with 2,460 men to capture Union supplies for the Confederacy. So well did the initial stages of the offensive go that on July 6, Hunt superseded the orders given him by General Bragg, his commanding officer, and crossed the Ohio River. He entered Indiana at the little town of Corydon. Morgan and his men proceeded north toward Indianapolis, moving through Palmyra and Salem on the way.

Panic ensued among the residents of Indiana, most of whom had never thought the war would reach out to threaten their security. The state militia was called out by the Governor and 60,000 men arrived in Indianapolis armed with shot guns, hunting rifles, and small arms to defend their state. Wisely deciding against attacking such a large defending force, General Morgan then turned his troops east through Versailles, Indiana, and on into Ohio where his troops were finally defeated and Morgan was captured on July 27. All told, Morgan had cut a swath four hundred miles long through the northern states. However, the raid itself was an additional disaster for the Confederacy. He had captured few supplies and his original force had dwindled to only three hundred men.

As fascinating as Indiana's short piece of Civil War history might be, there is a footnote to Morgan's raid that has produced an inexplicable consequence. As the old tale is told, while riding through Versailles one young officer from Morgan's company deserted. Some say that he was simply tired of the war and bloodshed he had seen in his tenure as a soldier. Others suggest that the young man was a native of Indiana, one of the few Hoosiers to wear the gray of the Confederacy during the war, who had no taste for attacking his native kinsmen. Whatever the case, all the stories agree as to his name: Silas Shimmerhorn.

After his hasty departure from the Confederate ranks, Shimmerhorn knew he was a hunted man. As a southern defector in a northern state, Shimmerhorn could well have been executed by either side had he been caught. For some time, he hid in the green hills, valleys, and woods outside of Versailles. Eventually, he happened upon the cavern now known as Bat Cave and adopted it as his new home.

His was a solitary, difficult life. At first, Shimmerhorn hunted game with the rifle he had retained from his time as a soldier. When his supply of bullets and gun powder dwindled, Shimmerhorn made a crude bow and set of arrows from tree branches. With these he hunted the game that was his only sustenance. Soon, however, he found strange company on his hunts.

At that time, packs of timber wolves still roamed the countryside and a particularly large pack frequented the area around Bat Cave. The stories say that instead of being fearful of the huge animals, Shimmerhorn befriended them with pieces of game that he had killed. Soon, Shimmerhorn was accepted as a member of the pack. As time passed, Shimmerhorn began to hunt with the pack, running wild through the fields at night in search of prey.

Emboldened by his new-found 'friends,' Shimmerhorn began to lead the pack on raids of local farms. Chicken houses were ransacked and cattle were slaughtered in the fields at night. Farmers were horrified to find their animals dead in the fields, their throats torn open by strong canine jaws, yet with portions of their meat carefully carved off as though by knife. Soon, stories began to circulate in the area about a wild man seen in the woods, accompanied by a pack of wolves. Farmers reported seeing an odd stranger standing at the edge of the woods silently watching them. If approached the man fled deep into the forest. He wore no shirt or shoes and his pants appeared to be nothing more than ragged remnants of a gray uniform. His hair and beard had grown long and wild and his eyes, they claimed, shone with a mad ferocity.

Eventually, residents began to set traps to catch the wild man. Farmers began to sit up all night, shotguns across their lap, in hopes of catching the man and his pack in one of their raids. However, it was all in vain. The Wolf Man of Versailles always proved too elusive for their traps. Trackers even traced the wolf pack back to Bat Cave but when the party neared their lair, they were suddenly confronted with a snarling wolves and were turned back.

Shimmerhorn became known as the 'Phantom of Bat Cave' and stories about him circulated throughout the community. It was even said that after the Civil War, a group of Shimmerhorn's old comrades rode north in order to find him and persuade him to return with them. They returned empty-handed with only the howl of a wolf pack echoing in their ears. But the days of the wolf pack and the strange phantom who accompanied them were fast fading away. More and more settlers were moving to the area. Forests that once served as the wolves' hunting grounds were chopped down to make way for more farms. With the passing years, the howls of the wolf pack began to disappear and the figure of the elusive Shimmerhorn was seen only infrequently.

Eventually, a posse of brave farmers dared to venture into Bat Cave. There they found the remnants of a pine straw bed and some rudimentary eating implements. Lying in one of the recesses of the cave they discovered a rusty confederate rifle with the initials 'SH' carved into the stock. But of the elusive Mr. Shimmerhorn, they could find no trace. The Phantom of Bat Cave was gone. The farmers heaved a collective sigh of relief.

Perhaps, however, their relief was a bit premature. Over the years, residents of the area have whispered tales that the Phantom of Bat Cave still walks the night. Farmers, coming home after a hard day's work, are startled by the sight of a phantom wolf pack running though the fields. In their midst is the figure of a strange man, his long hair and beard flowing around him like a cloak. The man and the pack are said to disappear from sight as quickly and mysteriously as they came.

One cave enthusiast is said to have run frightened from Bat Cave when, exploring its dark recesses, he suddenly came upon a strange man with long hair and fiery eyes, who stared threateningly at the young man for a moment and then vanished. As one outdoor writer put it, "Occasionally, even yet, campers at Versailles State Park during the darkest hours of the night hear the low, distant cry of a wolf pack, and occasionally report seeing a little old man with a long flowing beard and white hair merge with the pack of timber wolves to roam and hunt through Ripley County."

Just the stuff of legend and folklore? Maybe. But, if you happen to be camping amid the wooded splendor of Versailles State Park on a moonlit night, do not be terribly surprised if you hear the distant cry of a wolf pack, or even see the inexplicable figure of a small man gliding through the dusk, the wolves his only companions. For it is said that on such nights Silas Shimmerhorn returns, to hunt once more with the phantom pack and silently tread the wooded paths. He is a part of the history of the area, a part of the night itself, and a permanent fixture of Indiana ghost lore.[15]

The Gray Lady of
Willard Library

Governor and Mrs. Robert D. Orr
on behalf of
The Trustees and Friends of Willard Library
request the pleasure of your company
at a High-Spirited Dinner Dance
to Celebrate the Library's 100th year and
in honor of its Resident Spirit,
the Lady in Gray
Friday, the eighteenth of October
nineteen hundred eighty five
seven o'clock in the evening
at Willard Library
$25.00 per person
Black Tie
(Long Gray Veil Optional)
Spirits available at cash bar
Reservations limited to 250
Valet Parking
Music by the Temple Airs

It is not every ghost that can boast of a formal dance held in their honor, let alone a gala hosted by the Governor of Indiana. But, such is the renown of the Gray Lady of Willard Library in Evansville, Indiana.

Opened in 1885, the Willard Library was the brainchild of local philanthropist Willard Carpenter. An entrepreneur and successful businessman in the Evansville area for many years, Carpenter dreamed of building a university for his beloved town. However, he quickly realized that even his considerable financial resources were not sufficient for so grand a project. Instead, Carpenter settled for erecting a strikingly ornate building at the corner of First Avenue and Division and endowing it as a public library 'for the use of the people of all classes, races and sexes, free of charge, forever.' It was a noble undertaking and it was only appropriate that the facility be named the 'Willard Library' after its founder and benefactor.

Today the library continues in the work that Carpenter set in motion over a century ago. Not affiliated with the county library system, the library is supported by Carpenter's endowment as well as by private grants and funds raised by the 'Friends of Willard Library.'

From the outside, Willard Library is a striking structure. Built in the Italianate-Gothic style, the massive two-story brick building features large windows and a classic Victorian tower at one corner. Inside, a visitor is treated to high ceilings and ornate appointments that speak of the gentility and beauty of a bygone era. The library's immense collections are housed in large rooms on the first and second floors, as well as the children's room in the basement. In its 110-year history, the library has amassed over 100,000 books and manuscripts including rare and valuable works.

If the stories that surround the Willard Library are to be believed, then sometime in its history the grand old building has collected something else as well. Something as old as a well-worn volume of literature and, in its own way, as elegant and genteel as the building that it inhabits: an enigmatic phantom known as the Gray Lady.

The first person to record an encounter with the spirit was a man who was a custodian in the library during the early 1930s. It was his custom to work until 10 p.m., then leave for the evening and return at 3 a.m. to fire the furnace in the basement in preparation for the next day's activities. One cold winter night, the custodian, carrying a flashlight, entered the building and made his way quietly to the basement boiler room. As he unlocked the door to the furnace area and entered, his flashlight shining on the floor to illumine his way, he nearly bumped into a figure standing near the door. Thinking it might be one of the transients who frequently slept in the area, the startled workman swept his light upward.

To his astonishment, the figure he saw before him was that of a female in a long dress with a gray shawl around her shoulders; an outfit reminiscent of the fashions of the nineteenth century. More shocking still, as the dumbfounded custodian stared at her, the figure seemed to melt away into the darkness. In a moment, she was gone and he stood alone and frightened.

Thus was born the legend of the Gray Lady. After his initial encounter with the strange phantom, the custodian began to see her more often. In this case, however, familiarity did not breed ease and he eventually quit his job rather than endure further encounters with the specter.

Throughout the succeeding years, a great many other people have reported experiences with the Gray Lady. She has been seen crossing the main staircase to the second floor, in the employees lounge, and in the imposing tower attached to the corner of the building. It was her appearance in the tower that caused some consternation with local police.

Twenty years ago, the library was fitted with motion detectors tied to an alarm system to alert police in case of a break-in. When the alarm went off, the alarm company notified the police and the director of the library. It was his responsibility to unlock the front door, allowing police access to the building. Frequently the motion detectors went off in the dead of night only to have subsequent searches of the building reveal the building to be empty and showing no signs of forced entry.

Late one night, having been awakened by such an alarm the director, Mr. Baker, arrived at the library to find a police patrol car waiting for him at the curb. As was their custom, one of the policeman entered the building with Mr. Baker, while the other officer stayed outside to catch anyone making a hasty exit. As on previous occasions, a search of the building was in vain. Despite a careful room-by-room inspection, no living person was found in the building. "It must be the motion detector in the basement," Mr. Baker explained. "Lately it seems to be going off by itself. We will have to have it replaced." Finally, their search over, the two men left by the front door, locked it, and returned to their cars.

When Mr. Baker and the police officer reached the squad car, they found the officer who had remained outside in an excited state. "Did you catch her?" he asked, shining his flood light toward the building. "Who?" replied the policeman who had just inspected the building. "There was no one in the building."

Exterior of the Willard Library, circa 1915.
Courtesy of Willard Library.

"Of course there is," came his comrade's reply. "There was a woman in a long dress in the tower. I saw her clearly in the window!"

"Maybe you saw the Gray Lady," joked Mr. Baker, thinking the policeman's imagination might have been affected by the old legends.

"Who are you talking about?" came the policeman's reply. Clearly, he had never heard the legend of the Gray Lady, of which he has now become a part.

Though the Gray Lady has been seen throughout the building, her favorite locale seems to be the children's section in the basement, not far from where she was first seen so many years ago. The woman who had the most prolonged and most frequent contact with the Gray Lady was the children's librarian, Margaret Maier, who worked in the library for fifty years before her death in 1989. In an interview conducted just prior to her death, Ms. Maier reported first seeing the ghost in the early 1950s while in the basement children's section with her assistant, Helen Kamm. Ms. Maier described the ghost in much the same way as the night custodian had years before—a woman dressed in a long skirt and blouse with a gray shawl wrapped around her shoulders.

Further, according to Ms. Maier, she was often seen standing among the bookshelves, or in the adjoining staff area, only to fade into thin air in an instant. At other times, she was heard rustling among the shelves in the early morning as the two women arrived for work.

Margaret Maier recalled how the two would often see a dark shadow moving among the stacks of books in the late afternoon—a shadow that remained after shades were pulled to eliminate the daylight coming through the windows. Footsteps were sometimes heard crossing the isles between the bookshelves, and at odd moments objects would disappear from plain view, only to be found later in an unlikely spot.

Despite her frequent appearances the Gray Lady did not cause any serious mischief. Indeed, she seemed gentle and elusive. Perhaps this explains why, instead of being fearful of the specter, Ms. Maier seems to have become almost fond of the her and the feeling seems to have been reciprocated. In fact it appears that in 1980 when the children's section of the library was temporarily closed for renovation the phantom is reported to have taken up temporary residence in the home Ms. Maier shared with her sister!

Ms. Maier told several co-workers that, during the time the children's section was closed up, strange manifestations began to occur in her home. Appliances turned themselves on and unexplained noises resounded through the house at night. The Gray Lady herself was seen moving from room to room in the house. On one occasion her form was seen by Ms. Maier and her sister as it silently glided through their front room. On another occasion a nephew, visiting for an afternoon, caught a glimpse of the figure of a woman in a long skirt climbing the stairs from the kitchen toward the upper floor bedrooms.

When the renovation was over and the children's area was reopened, the migratory spirit ceased her manifestations in Mrs. Maier's home and began to be seen in the library once more. However, Ms. Maier's relationship with the apparition of the library continued unabated. During her tenure at the Willard Library, she seems to have developed an affinity for the Gray Lady. Far from being fearful of the ghost, Ms. Maier apparently came to see herself as the protector and spokesperson for her. When a local newspaper printed an article on the ghost, spelling her name in the title as "The Lady in Grey," Ms. Maier remarked to a co-worker, "My, they've misspelled her name!" In 1989, Ms. Maier retired from the library after fifty years of service. Several months later, she died. However, the spirit of the Gray Lady has stayed behind, despite the departure of her benefactor. In the succeeding years, a great many patrons and workers at Willard Library have claimed experiences with the Gray Lady.

One day shortly after beginning work at the library, librarian Joan Elliot came face-to-face with the Gray Lady descending the stairs toward the staff lounge. "I read on my breaks," she now recalls, "so I had a book in front of me. I was going down to the basement of the library into the boiler room and I had the sensation that there was someone right in front of me — you know, like you are going to run into them or something. I stopped, looked up and there was this lady in gray. I closed my eyes, and said, 'Wait a minute' and when I opened my eyes again, she was gone. She was very, very real to me."

Shortly thereafter, Ms. Elliot had another encounter with a strange phenomenon in the staff lounge. One day, on break once again, Ms. Elliot was in the staff restroom. Since there was just one restroom for both men and women, she carefully locked the door, and made her way to a stall. While in the bathroom stall, she was shocked to hear the sound of the water in the sink suddenly being turned on full force. Hesitantly, Ms. Elliot called out, but no reply was forthcoming. Ms. Elliot peered out of the stall to find the water running in the sink with both faucets turned on full. However, a quick search revealed the door was still locked and the small bathroom was empty.

This was not the only instance of the Gray Lady showing a propensity for turning on water. Betty Miller, while she was head librarian of the Willard Library, also had a unsettling experience of a similar kind. Since the library is traditionally closed on Mondays, Ms. Miller would sometimes come in on that day to work undisturbed. One day, when she knew she was alone in the building, she was interrupted in her work by the sound of running water coming from a utility room sink on the second floor. As she climbed the stairs toward the room to investigate, the sound ended as abruptly as it began. Quickly she entered the utility room to find it empty, but the sink wet with water. A search of the library from top to bottom only confirmed that the doors were locked, and no other living person was inside its walls.

Other manifestations have been of a more dramatic nature. Mrs. Anne Wells, the current children's librarian, has reported semi-regular experiences with the phantom. "My first experience with the ghost," she recounts, "was, appropriately, on Halloween day of 1993. I was working in the stacks when suddenly I became aware of this strong and strange aroma. It was an old scent . . . Sort of like patchouli. It is an old-fashioned perfume—a musk-based scent. Sort of like a smoky aroma—not so much a smell it was an aroma. It was strange because you could take two steps away from the area where I was standing and there would be no aroma at all, and then take two steps forward and the aroma would be very strong. I had my assistant with me and she smelled it too. Then it would suddenly disappear—it was like turning a light on or off."

Mrs. Wells reports that the odd smell has returned occasionally over the years. Others have also reported the scent as well. A member of a local genealogy society, alone in the library at night working on microfilm records, went to the staff bathroom to find the room filled with a smell "like an old perfume." The encounters with the strange aroma continue today. Like the spirit itself, it is a gentle, elegant scent, here one moment and gone the next.

Still other odd occurrences have been reported in recent years and Mrs. Wells was alone in the children's stacks shelving books. She wore a pair of earrings that she had recently purchased. "They were long, dangly earrings," she says. "They had Indian beads on them. They were really interesting to look at." As Mrs. Wells bent over to shelve some books, she felt a hand pull back her hair, as though to examine her earrings. "I thought maybe a child had come in and was looking at my earrings," she now recalls, "but when I turned around, there was no one there. There was no one in the whole basement."

Mrs. Well's assistant, Anita Glover, has also had several unexplained experiences at the library. Although she flatly claims to be a skeptic on all matters ghostly, she recounts several instances that have tested her skepticism. The first occurred as she glanced at a security monitor located in the children's room. "I was working here one day at my desk. We have TV monitors hooked up to security cameras so that we can see the halls. I looked at the monitor showing the basement hall and there was something moving. Everything else in the monitor was clear except this form. I could not tell if this was a man or woman — it was fuzzy — out of focus. It was there and moving, but then it just disappeared."

The most striking manifestation of the ghost's presence came about three years ago and began with a visit from a local kindergarten class. As Mrs. Wells tells the story, kindergarten classes frequently visit the children's section for a tour and story-telling. "I was going to do a story hour, but the kids asked me to tell them about the ghost instead. So I did — I told them the old legends that everybody knew about the Gray Lady. They got really excited and naturally on the way home the kids scared each other with the stories."

"Apparently, one of the children got pretty scared because the next day I got a phone call from a very upset parent. She complained that I had scared her child. I didn't like that — I had a daughter in kindergarten at that time, and I don't scare kids." Realizing that she had a potential public relations problem on her hands, Mrs. Wells called her staff together. She informed them of the situation and asked that from then on they be more careful about dispensing the legends of the Gray Lady to the public. "Let's just not be so open," she told her staff.

What happened next is forever etched into the memory of all concerned. The very next day, a woman from the community, who apparently was well versed in the legend of the Willard Library ghost, came to the children's section. Approaching Ms. Glover, who was shelving books at the time, she inquired if there had been any recent sightings of the Gray Lady.

Remembering her supervisor's request, Ms. Glover replied "Oh, no. We do not think that she is here anymore." As though on cue, at that moment a book on the top shelf seemed to jump off the bookcase, arced through the air and fell to the floor directly between the two women. Staring down at the book for a moment, Ms. Glover glanced back at the woman and replied cheerily, "Well, maybe I am mistaken because maybe she really is here!"

The sightings of the Gray Lady continue. Through the years, a large number of visitors and staff of the Willard Library have encountered strange experiences, especially in the basement children's section and adjacent staff area. The story of the Gray Lady has become part of the Willard Library's ambiance. In 1985, the Friends of the Library even held a fund-raising dinner dance in her honor, hosted by no less a personage than the Governor of Indiana himself. From all accounts, the Gray Lady declined the attention given her and was not in attendance.

Although her presence seems to be well-documented, her identity still remains a mystery. Through the years, the theory has developed that the spirit might be that of Louise Carpenter, daughter of library founder, Willard Carpenter. Later in life, Louise Carpenter, who felt cheated when her father left the bulk of his estate to the library endowment fund, initiated legal proceedings against the library to recover the funds that she felt were rightfully hers. Her attempt was futile, but to the end of her days, Louise Carpenter harbored a bitterness toward the library.

On the face of it, such a story might well explain the presence of a spirit in the library. Those, however, who know the legends best reject such an explanation. "I don't believe that," says Anita Glover, "because Louise Carpenter would be vengeful, but this ghost is not that." Betty Palmer, a staff member who has made a hobby of collecting stories of the Gray Lady, concurs. "There is nothing here that suggests an angry spirit," says Ms. Palmer. "The legend suggests a ghost that is more amiable and gentle."

Whoever or whatever it is that inhabits Willard Library does indeed seem gentle and elusive. Listening to the old and new stories, one gets the impression not of an angry specter rattling chains and moaning, but of a gentle spirit walking the floors at all hours of the day and night, shy and yet subtly mischievous.

As one staff member put it, "I guess we will never really know who or what it is that haunts these halls. But whoever she is, she is a part of us—a part of Willard Library, just a charming piece of this very charming place."

Perhaps no better epitaph could be offered any person— living or dead.

It is not every ghost that can boast of a formal dance held in their honor, let alone a gala hosted by the Governor of Indiana. But such is the renown of the Gray Lady of Willard Library in Evansville Indiana. So put on your black tie, bring your invitation, and come meet the Lady in Gray. But you may want to check your 'Miss Manners' before you decide on the proper form of greetings for the dead – it might go ill for you if you insulted the guest of honor![16]

EPILOGUE

The fire burns low and the embers glow in the darkness. The wind whispers among the trees bringing with it a damp cold as from the grave. The witching hour slowly fades and a new day begins. It is time, it seems, for us to part ways.

Thank you for sharing this campfire with me this evening. It has been a privilege to share some tales with you. Who knows but that we might share another fire on another night and tell other tales as well?

In the meantime, it is my hope that you have enjoyed our time together. May you have safe travel as you journey back to the "real world" and the safety of your bed. However, as you do, be reminded of the closing words of the play "Dracula" . . .

"Sleep well, but remember . . . there are such things."
MMW, All Hallows Eve, 1996

Acknowledgements

This book truly could not have been written without the help of a great many people, who gave of their time and assistance. A very special thanks to my dear friend Mr. Mike Carniello, who edited this work and contributed of his own considerable talent. Thanks Killer.

I wish to thank Mrs. Mary Mitsos, Librarian extraordinar, who helped with this project a long time before it was a project. Thanks to my long suffering secretaries, Mrs. Margo Tanner and Mrs. Joyce Dudeck, who worked on the manuscript and contributed their insights. Thanks to those who have participated in the Hoosier Folklore Project in collecting these stories, especially Mr. Larry Wirtz and Mrs. Jennifer Seniew Lantz. Thanks to my dear friends and skilled photographers, Mr. Chris Shultz and Ms. Kris Harrison, for the donation of their talents. A special thanks also to Mr. and Mrs. Bill Wilkins, who helped with the research and the manuscript of this work. Thanks to Dr. Douglas Zale, for his encouragement and friendship, and for never wavering in his belief that this project would bear fruit. Thanks to all who contributed their stories to this work- I hope you enjoy hearing your stories again. Thanks especially to the kind staff of Sigma Pi Fraternity, Willard Library, and Versailles State Park, as well as to the University of Notre Dame Archives department and the St. Mary of the Woods College Public Relations Department.

Thanks to Mrs. Chris Woodyard, writer, publisher, and friend. I owe you more than I can repay for helping make this dream a reality. Thanks to Maureen Morris, my editor at Thunder Bay. Finally the author wishes to convey a very special thank-you to Mr. J. Michael Norman, for his kindness and inspiration, as well as contributing information for this book.

Sources

1) *Haunted Heartland* by Beth Scott and Michael Norman, Stanton and Lee Publishers, 1985: 75-82. *Dunes County Magazine*, Winter 1982. Personal interviews, correspondence, and research.

2) *Haunted Heartland*: 82-83. "Stiffy Green" by Ronald L. Baker, in *Indiana Folklore Journal*, Indiana University Center for Language Sciences, Bloomington, Indiana, Volume III, #1, 1970: 113-127. Personal interviews, correspondence, and research.

3) *Notre Dame Observer*, March 4, 1983: 8-10. *South Bend Tribune*, March 11, 1990: D1. First hand accounts from the University of Notre Dame Archives. Personal interviews, correspondence, and research.

4) From "Toast to Foley Hall,"by Rosemary Nudd, SP. Used with permission.

5) "The Ghost of Foley Hall"in *Indiana Folklore Journal*, Volume I, #2, 1975: 117-123. *Woods Magazine*, October, 1975. Personal interviews, correspondence, and research.

6) *The Ghostly Register*, Arthur Myers, Contemporary Books, 1986: 126-129. Personal interviews, correspondence, and research.

7) Personal interviews, correspondence, and research.

8) Personal interviews, correspondence and research.

9) Personal interviews, correspondence, and research.

10) *Haunted Heartland*: 85. "The Negro in Concrete," Linda Deigh, in *Indiana Folklore Journal*, Volume I, #1, 1968: 61-67. "The Haunted Bridges Near Avon and Danville and Their Role In Legend Formation," Linda Deigh, in *Indiana Folklore Journal*, Volume II, #1, 1969: 44-89. Personal interviews, correspondence, and research.

11) *Haunted Heartland*: 112-115. "The Ghost of Cline Avenue," Philip Brandt George, in *Indiana Folklore Journal*, Volume V, #1, 1972: 57-91. Personal interviews, correspondence, and research.

12) Personal interviews, correspondence, and research.

13) Personal interviews, correspondence, and research.

14) *Haunted America*: 116-119. "The Legend of Stepp Cemetery," William M. Clements and William E. Lightfoot," in *Indiana Folklore Journal*, Volume V, #1, 1972: 92-131.

15) "The Legend of Bat Cave," Tom March, in *Outdoor Indiana*, November, 1964: 20-21. Personal interviews, correspondence, and research.

16) *A Ghosthunters Guide*, Arthur Myers, Contemporary Books,1993: 81-92. Personal interviews, correspondence, and research.

Final Note

The Hoosier Folklore Project is interested in collecting more stories of ghosts and hauntings in Indiana. If you have a story you might be willing to share, please contact hhproj@juno.com, or Mark Marimen, P.O. Box 837, Crown Point, Indiana 46307.